I0448653

TABLE OF CONTENTS

ILLUSTRATIONS

INTRODUCTION

> There can be no question of a purely military evaluation of a great strategic issue, nor of a purely military scheme to solve it.
>
> — Carl von Clausewitz

The creation of an effective and stable nation state following conventional conflict depends upon a careful and deliberate transition. The utilization of military power in state intervention comes with challenges beyond that of enemy focused military objectives. The restoration and enabling of legitimate governments following conventional military operations finalizes policy objectives. Therefore, United States (U.S.) policy directives and military doctrine emphasize the equal importance of conflict and stability operations in state interventions.[1] However, the marriage and transition between the two environments is often difficult. The pivotal transition period is a complex and uncertain environment that has evolved from the conflict itself. This requires a reevaluation and critical analysis of the transition period within its own context and meaning.

The recent interventions in Iraq and Afghanistan by the United States military serve to highlight the difficulty in fully understanding the elements of conflict transition and its scope and complexity. The continuing inability of the involved stakeholders to understand the operational scope of this transition period contributes to the misallocation of priorities and resources. This frustrates the efficient transformation of operational military successes into enduring strategic and policy victories. U.S. policy guidance and strategic planning priorities continue to pursue avenues to better capitalize on this transition and set optimal conditions towards achieving national policy objectives.

---

[1] U.S. Department of Defense, Department of Defense Directive (DODD) 3000.5, *Stability Operations* (Washington, DC: US Government Printing Office, 2004), 2. Directive 3000.5 specifically established that stability operations would be of equal prioritization as combat operations.

Our planning envisages forces that are able to fully deny a capable state's aggressive objectives…this includes being able to secure territory and populations and facilitate a transition to stable governments on a small scale for a limited period.[2]

As the historical reviews of conflict transformation will reveal, this visionary intent is still unrealized. This 'facilitation' of transitioning to a stable government continues to have trouble in integrating stakeholders under a shared understanding towards a mutually agreed upon end state.

The U.S. military planning for conventional operations in the realm of conflict has proven successful in decisively defeating the conventional enemy forces. This planning framework (to include joint force application) is adequate in the conventional engagement against structured forces. However, if the current U.S. planning frameworks are a tool for both conflict and stability producing environments, why have post conflict situations continued to frustrate effective operational planning? Are the components of security and resource allocation the primary determinants of success or failure? Are the historical planning frameworks and problem framing sufficient to understand the complexity and character of a society as it transitions from conflict to post conflict priorities? This monograph argues that the understanding of the concept of transition, the integration of stakeholders and an appreciation of contextual influences are critical to effecting positive change in the transition process.

The purpose of this monograph is to determine the character of conflict transition and particular influences that affect the conversion from conventional conflict to peacekeeping operations. This consideration of the nature of conflict to stability transitions will enable stakeholders to better prepare and manage long-term solutions towards stability. This in turn may allow the international community to improve approaches at stabilizing post conflict nations.

---

[2]Office of the Secretary of Defense, *Sustaining U.S. Global Leadership: Priorities for 21st Century Defense,* 5 January 2012, http://www.defense.gov/news/Defense_Strategic_ Guidance.pdf (accessed on 20 December 2012): 4.

This monograph is limited in scope and premised on several assumptions. The characteristics defining a post conflict transition are as varied to individual nations as they are to the internal and external factors that influence it. Material elements and the allocation of resources are a critical component of the transition process. Material areas include the resourcing of law enforcement and security forces, infrastructure rebuilding, essential services support and the operations of the intervening military forces. For example, the requirement to provide physical security in the operational area following conflict is often a necessity. The reviewed case studies offer insight to the transition phase but do not provide a complete historical review of the intervention or specific actions to be taken by involved stakeholders. The limited scope of this analysis does not intend to minimize the importance of the utilization of resources in the promotion of stability in the aftermath of conflict. However, the conceptual understanding of particular cognitive and framing elements that make up the operational environment should assist in the implementation of those material resources.

The successful outcome of the post conflict transition requires not only the shared understanding and integration of the invested stakeholders, but also the appreciation of the contextual, cultural and societal influences within the transition phase. The continued improvement upon operational approaches towards transition dictates a reassessment and analysis of current definitions, methodologies and conceptual frameworks used in post conflict transitions. Historically transition planning and implementation of stability measures have revealed limitations in holistically capturing the context of what a transition consists of and what elements influence its optimal outcome. This monograph will explore the elements of the transition and present the requirement for increased consideration of the post conflict environment.

Method

This monograph is an exploratory study of the transitional period following conflict. It is an effort designed to develop a more comprehensive approach towards appreciating the transition period between conflict and peacekeeping. The evaluation of the critical influencing elements in the post conflict period will draw from social and historical studies. It will first review the doctrinal and referenced definition of the transition period as expressed by the interested stakeholders of the transitional process. This review will be limited to the U.S. government, primarily the U.S. Department of Defense and State and associated agencies. It will additionally consider academic research and review the analysis of the transition in context. The monograph will then review the integration efforts of the involved stakeholders in improving performance in addressing the transition period. The evaluation will initially focus on the integration of U.S. governmental elements involved in state and conflict interventions. This mitigation of institutional barriers between U.S. stakeholders facilitates an effective integration of all the regional and international stakeholders.

The additional influencers of conflict transition will concentrate on the elements of power and culture within the environment. Recommendations on the use of holistic and systems thinking based approaches in incorporating these influences will be briefly considered. The case studies of the interventions in Iraq and Panama will serve to highlight specific insights in historical transitions from collapsed states progressing towards stability. The environments in Iraq and Panama introduce possible variables to the holistic appreciation of the transition in context and provide support for the formulation of a better appreciation for the transition period. The final chapter will conclude with an assessment of the current evaluation of the transitional period and provide recommendations to guide future research and policy development.

DEFINING THE TRANSITIONAL SECURITY GAP

There have been over twenty major operations by the international community to stabilize post-conflict nations with different strategies yielding a wide range of results in the last twenty years.[3] The U.S. militarily continues to produce operational military victories over oppositional forces in the field. These operational successes do not guarantee the stabilization of post conflict societies and government. In the intervention of Iraq in 2003, the inability of the Coalition nations to consolidate political and social arrangements in the intervening period of the transition witnessed the slow progression towards an enduring insurgency. The transition period is the pivotal cognitive and operational bridge that must facilitate the desired end state of a wide range of actors. As the transition period between these two environments is often ambiguous to both intervening forces and the populace of the host nation, it is therefore a critical first step in viewing the post conflict transition in its own character and context.

There must be a clear understanding of the operational environment and desired end state in post conflict transitions in order for planning to be effective. In the conflict environment, the populations of nations undergo a period of heightened anxiety. As the conflict resolves itself, this anxiety lessens for a period and then based on situational and environmental conditions will fluctuate. This period of time or "transition gap" provides an opportunity in which interagency and international actors can implement a reassessed analysis based on previous planning. Alternatively, this transition period can provide an opportunity for "spoilers" or actors working counter to desired stable end states and exploit transitional conditions for their own self-interests. This pivotal shaping period provides the *initial* and possibly best opportunity in which to outline the conditions toward a desired end state and prevent instability agents from establishing

---

[3]Nicholas J. Armstrong and Jacqueline Chura-Beaver, *Harnessing Post-Conflict Transition: A Conceptual Primer*, (Carlisle, PA: BiblioGov, 2010), vii.

5

themselves. The first step in harnessing this transitional period is forming a shared understanding of what characterizes and influences this process.

The transition between conflict and stability continues to resist a common understanding in both policy and military communities. Policy makers, scholars, international organizations and military professionals often define the concept of transition differently. This prevents a precise understanding of what characterizes a transition between conflict and stability. In order to appreciate this range of definition, a review of the concept of transitions by military planners, policy makers and the academic community is necessary.

The U.S. Joint doctrine-phasing model and U.S. Army doctrine contain distinctions in the concept of transitions. Joint publication 3–0 states:

> A phase is a definitive stage of an operation or campaign during which a large portion of the forces and capabilities are involved in similar or mutually supporting activities for a common purpose. Phasing, which can be used in any operation regardless of size, helps the Joint Force Commander organize large operations by integrating and synchronizing subordinate operations.[4]

This phasing construct assists the military planner's ability to tailor operational resources to specific environments within the operation. Transitions within this planning construct are the linkage points between the phasing construct in Joint doctrine. Figure 1 outlines this planning framework.

---

[4]US Department of Defense, Joint Publication (JP) 3–0, *Joint Operations* (Washington, DC: Government Printing Office, 11 August 2011), xvii. See also Joint Publication (JP) 5–0, *Joint Operations Planning* for a more detailed description of the phasing construct used in the phased planning model.

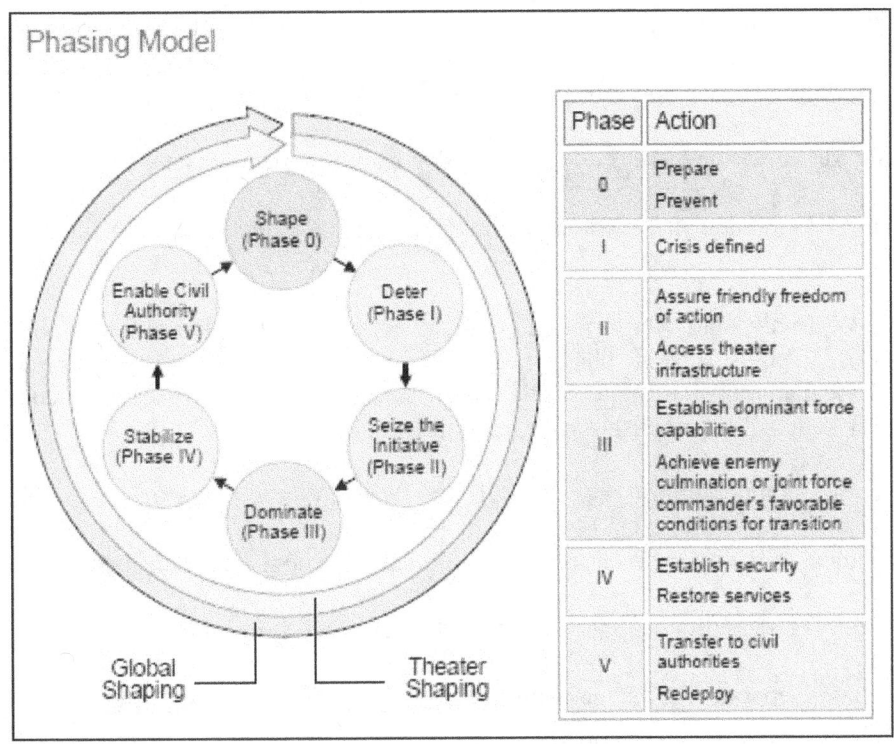

Figure 1. Joint Phasing Model, August 2011

Source: US Department of Defense, Joint Publication (JP) 3–0, *Joint Operations*

The phasing construct cognitively frames the operational environment and assists commanders in weighting resources of defense, offensive and stability operations throughout the campaign. The phasing construct is linear in nature and entails six phases ranging from Shape (Phase 0) to Enabling Civil Authorities (Phase V). Phase III is considered the "Dominate Phase" in which the joint force employs resources to engage and defeat (culminate) an opposing force and then transition to the follow on phase, Phase IV (stabilize). The Joint Force Doctrinal phasing model is a useful one in prioritizing the allocation of resources under a joint environment. The phasing model is not argued here as an ineffective model for organizational planning. However, a further analysis of the transition bridging Phase III and IV will reveal additional operational opportunities bridging the two phases.

The transition from kinetic to non-kinetic population centric operations is a dynamic and contextual reorientation of the application of national and military power. In Joint Publication 3–0 and supporting joint doctrine there is an emphasis that stability operations are the dominant feature of Phase IV planning and operations. However, this has come under some criticism:

> Phase IV usually starts very soon after the advent of combat in Phase III, and the two overlap…Even the separate phasing itself might be worth rethinking, as the construct can stovepipe planning and hamper the holistic vision necessary to properly link combat to the end state that accomplishes national political objectives.[5]

The conversion period bridging Phase III and Phase IV in joint military planning is a distinct realignment of the operational focus. Additionally, the conflict has influenced the contextual, cultural and environmental conditions. This requires a reevaluation of the operational environment that is separate and distinct from the previous planning phase. Linear planning within the joint phasing construct may disregard or miss sight of opportunities or spoilers within the transition phase. The second and third order effects of this mismanagement of the transition phase could affect future stability operations.

A careful look at the phasing model for joint operations reveals that the Phase III (dominate) transition to Phase IV (stabilize) is a radical shift in prioritization. "The stabilize phase is typically characterized by a shift in focus from sustained combat operations to stability operations."[6] The shift in focus from inherently kinetic combat operations to that of stability focused operations is the most drastic and diametric shift in the planning and allocation of resources. In the transitioning period, it is of critical importance to adequately reassess the operational environment within the transition period and realign previous planning estimates. The

---

[5]Conrad C. Crane, "Phase IV Operations: Where Wars are Really Won, Turning Victory into Success: Military Operations after the Campaign," *Military Review* (May-June 2005): 27-36.

[6]JP 3–0, *Joint Operations*, V-9.

joint planning framework and its linear progression do not properly emphasize this necessary focus on the temporal gap bridging the two operational environments.

Joint Force doctrine defines transitions between phases as distinct shifts in focus of operations, often accompanied by changes in command or support relationship and priorities of effort. The activities that occur during a given phase, however, rarely align with neatly definable breakpoints. Planners cannot define the complexity of the regional factions, environment, security situation, and population sentiment at the cessation of hostilities with precision. This phasing structure does not appreciate the conflict to stability period in its own context.

Several studies on the intervention in Iraq and Afghanistan properly weight the importance of this temporal gap in the transition phase. The RAND Corporation, in a 2005 study titled, "Establishing Law and Order after the Conflict," characterized this transition period as the golden hour.

> First, establishing security during the golden hour should be the most immediate concern of policymakers after the conclusion of major combat operations. This golden hour is a time frame of several weeks to several months, during which the external intervention may enjoy some popular support and international legitimacy, and when potential spoilers may have insufficient time to organize.[7]

The transition phase between Phase III and Phase IV operations must account for this "golden hour" in the joint planning model. The U.S. Army is continuing to review its planning frameworks for effectively approaching the transitioning between these operational environments. The newly implemented Unified Land Operations doctrine by the U.S. Army better accounts for this transitional temporal period and the opportunities within it. The U.S. Army Decisive Action doctrine outlines this reconsidered approach.

---

[7]Seth G. Jones, *Establishing Law and Order After Conflict* (Santa Monica, CA: Rand Publishing, 2005), 1–2. The term "golden hour" is a term to illustrate the time period following an injury that treatment is most critical to save a patient.

Decisive action is not a phasing method. Commanders consider the concurrent conduct of each task—offensive, defensive, and stability or defense support of civil authorities—in every phase of an operation.[8]

Throughout a military campaign, the commander elevates priority to stability operations as necessary. When environmental or operational conditions change, the commander makes the proper adjustments to the tasks within the concept of ongoing operations. Mission Command and the Army Design Methodology assist the commander in correctly reframing the post conflict problem set and realigning operational priorities to best support the progress of stability. The critical linkage of this reframing involves correctly assessing when the transition is approaching, when it has initiated and how long it will last. Army doctrine addresses this important element in its newly implemented doctrinal publications Army Doctrine Reference Publication (ADRP) 3–0 *Unified Land Operations* and ADRP 3–07 *Stability*.

According to U.S. Army doctrine, transitions "mark a change of focus between phases or between the ongoing operation and execution of a branch or sequel...a shift in relative priority between the elements of full spectrum operations."[9] As conditions change, commanders adjust priorities based on actual or anticipated situations and assign or reassign resources. In this planning construct, the transition is a reorientation of a decisive point on a line of effort. ADRP 3–07, *Stability*, a supporting doctrinal document to the ADRP 3–0, *Unified Land Operations* provides greater clarity on the U.S. doctrinal scope of the transition:

Transitions mark a change of focus between phases or between the ongoing operation and execution of a branch or sequel. This shift in relative priority between the elements of decisive action—such as from offense to stability—also involves a transition. Transitions require planning and preparation well before their execution. The staff identifies potential transitions during planning and accounts for them throughout execution; assessment

---

[8]U.S. Department of the Army, Army Doctrine Reference Publication (ADRP) 3–0, *Unified Land Operations* (Washington, DC: Government Printing Office, May 2012), 2–7.

[9]U.S. Department of the Army, Army Doctrine Publication (ADP) 3–07, *Stability*, (Washington, DC: Government Printing Office, 31 August 2012), 3–5.

ensures that the staff measures progress toward such transitions and takes appropriate actions to prepare for and execute them. In a stability context, operations can involve multiple types of transitions and often occur concurrently.[10]

This definition provides the temporal range of the transition and its relational role to ongoing operations. It additionally identifies planning requirements to best support it. The description includes the need for ongoing assessments and the identification of transitional indicators. However, the definition does not capture the elements within the transition phase. This absence of a dedicated conceptual snapshot of the transition phase may cede operational opportunities with it. The elements within the transition phase will have changed at the termination of hostilities. The reframing of the operational environment is required in order to appreciate the new contextual influences of the transition.

U.S. Army doctrine provides a better understanding of the post conflict transition in regards to planning considerations and the need to realign priorities in response to a changed environment. While adequate in defining the actions and priorities of the force, there is an absence of the critical dynamic elements within the transition phase. The failure to address the transition as a conceptual separate element from the next phase or operational line may result in counterproductive implementation of effort. This may include mission creep, leveraging improper elements of governmental control and disruption of the social climate. The holistic understanding of the interrelationships in the environment is important. "Everything is connected to everything else."[11] In the post conflict period, interrelationships of the involved actors undergo an evolution of connectively. These connections can become compromised, altered or even broken. It is therefore vital that military doctrine incorporates an appreciation of the holistic elements within

---

[10]Ibid., 3–5.

[11]Lt. Gen. Anthony Zinni, "Lt. Gen. Zinni's Twenty Lessons Learned for Humanitarian Assistance and Peace Operations," (Center for Naval Analysis Annual Conference Proceedings: Military Support to Complex Humanitarian Emergencies, 1995), 5.

the transition phase. A review of the State Department and academic community characterizations of transition highlight this requirement.

The Bureau of Conflict and Stabilization Operations (CSO), the U.S. State Department's lead proponent in post-conflict support, utilizes a number of documents in supporting nations emerging from conflict. In one of their establishing documents, *Guiding Principles for Stability and Reconstruction*, CSO outlines the transitional environment in a more holistic fashion:

> Post-conflict environments are characterized by high volatility. Needs may change (new population displacements, for example); priorities may change (subsequent realization that a marginalized region or population segment poses a risk for peace building if their needs are not addressed); national counterparts may change, with implications for their views on recovery priorities; reforms or capacity building may prove to be more difficult than originally envisaged, necessitating changes in timing; the composition of the donor or international support group may change; and costs of reconstruction may change, due to security conditions or changes in possible sources of supply of materials or services.[12]

The CSO acknowledges the challenges in the transition process and attempts to frame this problem set in a dynamic way. "The successful transition from conflict to sustainable peace involves managing change through constant learning and calibration of strategies to particular country circumstances that are always in flux."[13] Successful transition involves managing change and calibrating strategies in response to an evolving environment. These strategies emphasize constant adaptation, locally led input in sequencing and timing of resource allocation, maximizing initial efforts and operations that are not linearity focus but based on integrated strategic vision and direction.[14] Members of the academic community further support this level of complexity.

Recently there has been resurgence on academic focus on post-conflict environments and the transition following conflict. Of particular interest to this study of the post conflict period,

---

[12]United States Institute of Peace, "Guiding Principles for Stabilization and Reconstruction (SSR)," *UNDP/WB, Draft Joint Guidance Note on Integrated Recovery Planning* (2009): 5–32, http:www.state.gov/j/cso/resources (accessed 16 November 2012).

[13]Ibid., 5-33.

[14]Ibid., 5-32.

Nicholas Armstrong explores the dichotomies of post conflict transitions in his publication, *Harnessing Post-Conflict Transitions: A Conceptual Primer*. Armstrong further partitions transitions and provides conceptual elements of its aims.

> Transition is inherently complex, and may include multiple, smaller-scale transitions that occur simultaneously or sequentially. These small-scale activities focus on building specific institutional capacities and creating intermediate conditions that contribute to the realization of long-term goals.[15]

Armstrong identifies six types of transitions documented in research literature. These transitions are war-to-peace, power, societal, political-democratic, security and economic. Each of these transitions involves specific characteristics that describe the underlying motivations impelling the transition. Armstrong's analysis of war-to-peace transitions further delineates the scope and scale of conflict-generated transformations.

Armstrong details that war-to-peace transitions encompass both inter- and intra-state conflict across global, regional and domestic levels of analysis. Traditional nation states and international organizations play a role in the management of intrastate conflicts and the transition to stability and peace efforts.[16] This responsibility encompasses an environment beyond the scope of solely governmental institutions and armed forces. As Armstrong notes, an understanding of the broad range and scope of stakeholders and typology of transition assist in developing a tailored approach to best capitalize on the transition period.

---

[15]Armstrong and Chura-Beaver, 13.

[16]For sources that further examine the elements of international actors in war-to-peace transitioning, see A. Bellamy and Williams, "Who's keeping the peace? Regionalization and Contemporary Peace Operations," *International Security*, 29, no.4; S.P. Campbell, "(Dis)integration, incoherence and complexity in UN post-conflict interventions," *International Peacekeeping*, 15, no. 4; W.J. Durch, "Peace and Stability Operations: Challenges and Opportunities for the Next U.S. Administration," (Washington, DC: Stimson Center, 2008); G.A. Dzinesa, "A comparative perspective of UN peacekeeping in Angola and Nambia," *International Peacekeeping*, 11, no. 4, (2004); N.M. Ripsman, "Two stages of transition from a region of war to a region of peace: Realist transition and liberal endurance," *International Studies Quarterly*, 49, no. 4.

The transition period is a procedural event following conventional conflict. The cessation of major combat operations followed by an indistinct period of uncertainty characterizes this environment. Definitive conflict or stability classifications do not adequately define the post-conflict transition phase. The actions of all stakeholders shape the transitional period in an evolved environment through dynamic and relational actions. The wide range of discourse and definition would suggest that the transition period is a dynamic contextual period that needs its own cognitive and conceptual framework. This conceptual framework should facilitate the planning review and reframing towards mutual stakeholder end states. The planning constructs of organizations such as the U.S. military can supplement current doctrine with a more integrated approach in how to approach the transition. Further research and study on the development of a workable conceptual framework that can be used and understood by a broad range of stakeholders is worthy of future consideration.

A review of the characterizations and definitions of the transition period by the involved actors in post conflict reveals several trends. U.S. military doctrinal considerations focus on the deliberations commanders must consider in prioritizing the allocation of resources and operations during transition periods. The State Department and its associated organizations further review and assess the transition as a period of complexity and interrelationships. Additionally, elements of the academic community further examine the transition period and reveal further distinctions in the levels of complexity, systems relationships and underlying motivations. It is therefore vital that military doctrine incorporates an appreciation of the integral elements within the transition phase. This will work towards incorporating a more holistic review of the transition period and enable a shared solution to a unique contextual problem. A review of how best to integrate contributing actors and appreciate the influencing elements in transition may reveal opportunities to enable this holistic and complementary approach.

INFLUENCES WITHIN THE TRANSITION

Integrating stakeholders and then implementing the most effective measures depends on a shared understanding of both the environment and the strategic vision of all actors. There are numerous challenges in transitioning from high intensity conflict to stability-focused operations. Every nation state or regional conflict comes with its own unique complex problem set. Political, ethnic and ideological motivations contribute to influencing the transition and its aftereffects. Accounting for the fluid transitioning environment requires a cognitive approach that can appreciate the complexity of a social system and its environment at multiple levels. The integration of the intervening agencies enables the positive participation of the population residing in conflict areas. The influences of power in the host nation and how external actors leverage power promote or undermine the stability process. The structure of culture and its effect on social resiliency in an uncertain environment affect the transition process. These components have complementary effects in the transition process and its promotion of long-term stability. This systems appreciation enables a more collaborative framework in the effective planning and reframing of the transition period. It is in the best interest of military and civilian planners to appreciate these elements of the transition period in order to improve upon enabling post conflict nations. This section will review the historical attempts at the integrating stakeholders and recommend an integrative planning approach to facilitate this shared interest.

Stakeholder Integration

Integrating all stakeholders in a post conflict environment is a critical component of the stability process. A shared vision and understanding of the post conflict environment facilitates a more comprehensive approach to achieving desired stability. Failure to incorporate all external and internal stakeholders will lead to misallocation of resources at best and resumption of conflict at worst. Lieutenant General William Caldwell emphasizes this integration in his introductory remarks of the Army stability doctrine, "we must strengthen the capacity of the other elements of national power, leveraging the full potential of our interagency partners" since military success "alone will not be sufficient to prevail."[17] This includes numerous governmental agencies of the intervening nations, non-governmental organizations, conflict nation governmental institutions and a myriad of social and cultural elements within the conflict nation itself. The integration of all stakeholders in the post conflict process begins with the collaboration of the intervention nation and its institutions. As recently as 2011, there has been a renewed emphasis for better integration of U.S. agencies in support of foreign policy objectives.

> To form better and more effective partnerships, we require more flexible resources, and less cumbersome process. We see authorities for a pooled-resources approach to facilitate more complementary efforts across departments and programs, integrating defense, diplomacy, development, law enforcement, and intelligence capacity building activities.[18]

However, despite national level directives and policy guidance, this integration continues to be a challenge. This chapter will review the historical efforts at interagency integration and offer recommendations to improve upon existing intent to improve interoperability.

Since 1997, the U.S. government has established evolving guidance in an attempt to improve upon the interagency ability to address post conflict integration and planning in interventions. Presidential Decision Directive (PDD) 56, under the Clinton Administration, emphasized the need of integrative planning frameworks and unity of effort by civilian and military agencies.[19] However, due to institutional and bureaucratic resistance the later Bush

---

[17]U.S. Army, Army Field Manual (FM) 3–07, *Stability Operations* (Washington, DC: Government Printing Office, 2008), forward.

[18]U.S. Joint Chiefs of Staff, *National Military Strategy of the United States* (Washington, DC: Government Printing Office, 2011), 15.

[19]Presidential Decision Directive/National Security Council 56, Managing Complex Contingency Operations, www.fas.org/irp/offdocs/pdd56/htm (accessed 4 February 2013), 2-3.

Administration rescinded it in 2001.[20] In 2003, during the intervention of Iraq, National Security Presidential Directive (NSPD-24) placed DoD in charge of post conflict reconstruction. The Office of Reconstruction and Humanitarian Assistance (ORHA) and later the Coalition Provisional Authority (CPA) led these stability efforts under DoD authority. In May of 2004, NSPD-36, transferred responsibility for reconstruction back to the State Department.

In 2005, National Security Presidential Directive 44 (NSPD-44) established the Department of State as the departmental lead in stabilization and reconstruction efforts by the U.S. in foreign interventions. This directive additionally offers guidance for military planners on how to best support stability operations as the supporting organization. The directive allows the Secretary of State to coordinate with the Secretary of Defense to integrate stability efforts regardless of the scope of conflict. It additionally directs the State Department to develop strategies to facilitate reconstruction and stabilization with all stakeholders that contribute to the effort.[21]

Under NSPD-44, the Department of Defense Directive (DODD) 3000.05 established the Defense Departments role in post conflict operational support. It outlines the Stability, Security, Transition and Reconstruction (SSTR) operations as activities that support U.S. efforts to promote sustainable peace while advancing U.S. interests. The directive further defines the role of the U.S. military as a supporting agency in these efforts towards policy objectives.[22] DODD 3000.05 additionally established the criteria that stability tasks were a core military function equal in prioritization as traditional combat tasks. One of the identified shortfalls of the directive is that it

---

[20]Nina M. Serafino, Peacekeeping/stabilization and Conflict Transitions: Background and Congressional Action On the Civilian Response/reserve Corps and Other Civilian Stabilization and Reconstruction Capabilities (Washington, DC: Congressional Research Service, 2012), 4.

[21]NSPD-44, www.state.gov/documents/organization/104099.pdf (accessed 21 October 2012).

[22]Department of Defense, Department of Defense Instruction (DODI) 3000.5, *Stability Operations* (Washington, DC: Government Printing Office, 2007), 4.

does not address the inability of all government agencies to integrate resources during planning and execution of U.S. interventions.[23] In 2009, Department of Defense Instruction (DODI) 3000.5 replaced DODD 3000.5 to address this resource shortfall and position the DoD in a position to take the lead in stability operations if necessary.

DODI 3000.5 highlighted the concern that civilian agencies should perform stability and nation enabling operations. The modification to DODD 3000.5 caveated that DoD "shall be prepared to lead stability operation activities" if the civilian agencies are not prepared or resourced. The three military functions in support of these stability operations were described as rebuilding host-nation institutions, revive or build the private sector and develop representational frameworks supporting host nation governments. Nonetheless, DODI 3000.5 emphasizes the need for close integration in intervention operations with the interagency community as well as the wider range of stakeholders with mutual interests in intervention outcomes.[24]

A significant obstacle to the realization of this directive and its intent were the resources available to the U.S. State Department. The initial lead agency within the State Department for post-conflict stabilization was the Office of the Coordinator for Reconstruction and Stabilization (S/CRS). In 2004, the State Department established S/CRS in response to intervention lessons learned in Operation Iraqi Freedom and Enduring Freedom. S/CRS establishing intent was to solve existing problems with the previous NSPD-24. S/CRS was to act as the primary State Department agency involved in post-conflict and stability situations.[25]

---

[23]Secretary of Defense, *Report to Congress on the Implementation of DODD 3000.05 Military Support for Stability, Security, Transition, and Reconstruction (SSTR) Operations*, (Washington, DC: Government Printing Office, 2007), i.

[24]Department of the Army, Army Doctrine Reference Publication (ADRP) 3–07, *Stability* (Washington, DC: Government Printing Office, 2012), 1–10-1–11.

[25]U.S. Department of State, "S/CRS Fact Sheet," www.state.gove/s/crs/rls/43327.htm (accessed 22 October 2012).

Despite encouragement from the DOD, the S/CRS struggled to achieve the objectives of its mission statement over the next five years. However, by 2010, the S/CRS had not developed an effective structure within the interagency community. The former coordinator, Ambassador John Herbst identified that "to date, S/CRS has not been given a principal role in any major crisis."[26] The lofty goal of the S/CRS notwithstanding, it is not the primary mechanism for conflict transformation or interagency bridge to facilitate enduring stability and reconstruction efforts immediately following conventional conflict.

In late 2010, the State Department released the Quadrennial Diplomacy and Development Review (QDDR) subsuming the S/CRS with the newly established Bureau for Conflict and Stabilization Operations (CSO). The new bureau's stated mandate is to "build upon and go beyond" the mandate and capabilities of S/CRS to facilitate the conflict prevention and stability transitioning.[27] This renewed effort and its success at integrating the national agencies remains questionable. The historical record of policy guidance in overcoming institutional barriers may indicate that subsequent efforts along the same lines will continue to be difficult.

In a 2005 article of *Military Review*, Conrad Crane highlighted one institutional difference of the organizations.

> The ironic truth about Phase IV (Stability) Operations is that the American military would rather not deal with them, or would like to quickly hand them off to other government agencies or international organizations, who in turn argue that the tasks associated with nation building are rightfully with their sphere of responsibility.[28]

---

[26]Naveed Bandali, "Coordinating Reconstruction and Stabilization: An Interview with Ambassador John E. Herbst (Ret.)," *Journal of International Peace Operations* 6, no. 4 (January-February 2011): 22.

[27]U.S. Department of State, "Quadrennial Diplomacy and Development Review," (2010), http://www.state.gov/documents/organization/15310.pdf (accessed on 04 November 2012), 136.

[28]Conrad C. Crane, "Phase IV Operations: Where Wars are Really Won," 27.

Crane further states that while there is a general agreement on who should be the lead in stability and reconstruction efforts, the military is the only organization with the resourcing and capabilities to conduct it.

The organization restructuring did not achieve its desired intent to integrate the interagency community in state interventions. The institutional resistance and resource shortfall proved to be difficult. In the post conflict, transition the integration of intervening organizations is the foundational element is incorporating a wider spectrum of regional and state actors. The development of a shared understanding towards desired end states and enabling planning processes may mitigate this institutional resistance. Planning frameworks that integrate effort (if not organizations) towards these shared objectives can provide the vehicle in which to enter the transition period. The S/CRS developed three such frameworks aimed at directly addressing the transitional gap between conflict and stability operations and better integrate stakeholders.[29] One of the frameworks is the Interagency Management System for Reconstruction and Stabilization (IMS).

The National Security Council approved the IMS for implementation in 2007. The was intended to provide decision makers at the policy and strategic level flexible options in which to enact planning processes for unified USG implementation. These plans included funding, joint interagency deployments, joint civilian operations and shared communication and information management architecture.

> S/CRS created the IMS, which while approved, has never really been used. Something like that could ensure that all the relevant players and agencies are brought together in an efficient process, but it has to be established and used.[30]

---

[29]U.S. State Department, "S/CRS Archive," U.S. State Department website, http://www.state.gov/j/cso/scrsarchive/index.htm (accessed 12 November 2012).

[30]Bandali, 22.

The IMS was a major first step in forming the strategic nexus of planning and execution for future crisis; however, the larger interagency community never embraced it.

Military and civilian agencies are the two governmental actors in a state intervention involving conflict and the transition to peacekeeping. The impact of the relational priorities that govern their interactions with each other is an additional consideration. The body of research drawing on historic case studies and polling data indicates that military and civilian agencies significantly differ on how best to use military force in supporting conflict transition and foreign policy.[31] Much research characterizes military agencies as conservative and territorial in organizational planning with a tendency to frame problem sets to maximize access to resources in addressing the policy challenge.[32]

Military operations are only a subset of the overall policy objectives in state interventions. The historical emphasis by military professionals has tended to weight focus on the military operations and neglect the stability and restoration process. Comments made by General Tommy Franks during the planning process for the 2003 Iraq War serve to illustrate this common tendency. "Keep Washington focused on policy and strategy. Leave me the hell alone to run the war."[33] The ineffective union of military and civilian agencies under a holistic and unified

---

[31]On the organizational and institutional preferences of soldiers and civilians, See Richard Betts, *Soldiers, Statesmen and the Cold War Crisis* (New York: Columbia University Press, 1991, original edition 1977); Peter Feaver, *Armed Servants: Agency, Oversight, and Civil-Military Relations* (Cambridge, MA: Harvard University Press, 2003), 58-75; Peter Feaver and Christopher Gelpi, *Choosing Your Battles: American Civil-Military Relations and the Use of Force* (Princeton: Princeton University Press, 2004); and Graham Allison and Philip Zelikow, *Essence of Decision: Explaining the Cuban Missile Crisis*, Second Edition (New York: Longman, 1999), 143-242.

[32]See Samuel Huntington, *The Soldier and the State: The Theory and Politics of Civil-Military Relations*, 79 and Jack Snyder, *The Ideology of the Offensive: Military Decision Making and the Disasters of 1914* (Ithaca: Cornell, 1984), 24.

[33]Hew Strachan, "Strategy or Alibi? Obama, McChrystal, and the Operational Level of War," *Survival*, 52:5 (2010): 440.

approach will continue to challenge the effective and optimal outcomes of the post conflict period until addressed.

In summary, the post conflict transition requires an integrated civilian and military cooperative effort. There appears to be much room for improvement in terms of current integration of interagency organizations. Recent governmental directives and restructuring have proven ineffective at overcoming the institutional and resource constraints of organizations with differing priorities. The transition period whereupon conflict priorities transform to conflict mitigation and stability is perhaps the most defining moment in state interventions. The policy goals and perspectives in the military and civilian realms is a significant challenge in effectively collaborating on effective planning and execution during the transition phase. Integrating conceptual environmental frameworks and developing overarching system thinking approaches towards strategic and policy end states may offer additional avenues in which to incorporate all stakeholders in a shared and cooperative understanding of the transition period. The answers to the integration of stakeholders lie not in the organizational structuring but rather in unified conceptual planning and projected end states towards condition setting in the post conflict period.

The Dynamics of Power in the Transition

The effective use of all elements of national and local power in transition phasing is important. U.S. agencies and the academic community prioritize, view and express the elements of national power differently. The holistic approach in post conflict transitions must additionally consider the influence of power within cultural and societal contexts. The limited studies that address power in transitions focus on power relations as predictors of conflict or the likelihood of stability in peaceful power transitions.[34] Further study on the elements of power and its

---

[34]For power relations as predictors of conflict see Steve Chan, "Exploring Puzzles in Power-Transitions Theory: Implications for Sino-American Relations," *Security Studies* 13, no. 3.

expression and its influence in the post war environment may assist in a more holistic understanding of this complex environment. This chapter will expand upon existing research of power and its linkage to post conflict to peacekeeping transitions.

The discussion of power within governments has traditionally conformed to two dichotomies, hard and soft power. Dr. Colin Gray, director for the Center for Strategic Studies, separates the expression of power into two realms. Hard power "is achieved through military threat or use, and by means of economic menace or reward."[35] Soft power, on the other hand is "the ability to have influence by co-opting others to share some of one's values and, as a consequence, to share some key elements on one's agenda for international order and security."[36] Both elements of hard and soft power influence the dynamics of the transition period.

Analyzing and harnessing the elements of power within the transition period can support establishing favorable conditions. Following war or conflict termination, the predominance of real power no longer resides in the military forces that have achieved military victory. Military power has expressed the elements of hard power in the defeat of the conventional forces. The dependence on the continued exercise of hard power following the post conflict phase will not ensure continued progress towards desired policy objectives. In the pursuit of policy objectives, that desire stability and a road to a legitimate government the other elements of power and their expression must reviewed and reformulated.

(2004) and Indra De Soysa, John Oneal, and Yee-Hee Park, "Testing Power-Transition Theory Using Alternative Measure of National Capabilities," *The Journal of Conflict Resolution,* Vol. 41. No.4 (1977). Discussion on peaceful power transition see Charles Kupchan, Jason Davidson and Mira Sucharov, *Power in Transition: The Peaceful Change of International Order* (Tokyo, Japan New York: United Nations University Press, 2001).

[35]Colin S Gray, *Hard Power and Soft Power: the Utility of Military Force as an Instrument of Policy in the 21st Century* (Carlisle, PA: Create Space Independent Publishing Platform, 2012), vii.

[36]Ibid.

As conventional conflict concludes the diffusion of power in the intervened nations, governmental and social structure undergoes an evolution. As broadly defined here, power is the capacity to do things and in societal situations to affect others to get desired outcomes. The conflict transition period and the follow on stability efforts depend on the elements of power in affecting others to achieve desired outcomes. The desired outcome within a post conflict environment is to promote social stability that promotes the evolution of legitimate government. This appreciation of power must consider both actors and their expression of power within their context. "Even when we focus primarily on particular agents or actors, we cannot say that an actor "has power" without specifying power "to do what?"[37]

Joseph S. Nye in *The Future of Power* posits that "power" is sometimes ambiguous and difficult to measure. This characterization holds true for the post conflict environment. Traditional indicators of power have evolved in the twenty first century. Strategies must include a wide range of power sources beyond that of the previous definition of a state's military strength. "We must specify who is involved in the power relationship (the scope of power) as well as what topics are involved (the domain of power)."[38] Context and relationships play another integral element to consider. "A policy-oriented concept of power depends upon a specified context to tell us who get what, how, where, and when."[39] The relationships of power undergo a transformation once conventional conflict has concluded and emergent actors recalibrate the equation progressing towards policy end states. The policy of the United States in the intervention may remain static (i.e. to impose a stable and legitimate government) however; the orientation of the

---

[37]Jack Nagel, *The Descriptive Analysis of Power* (New Haven, CT: Yale University Press, 1975), 14.

[38]Joseph S. Nye, *The Future of Power* (Public Affairs: Perseus Books Group, 2011), ix-xii.

[39]Thomas X, Hammes, *The Sling and the Stone: On War in the 21ˢᵗ Century* (St. Paul, MN: Zenith Press, 2004), 31.

policy must undergo transformation in regards to the approach how to leverage the influencers of power in the post-conflict environment. The contextual and knowledgeable conversion of power resources and the obtainment of desired outcomes are dependent upon effective leadership and well-designed planning frameworks.[40]

In the transition environment, hard power must give way to a softer form of power expression. The preferred outcome in a post conflict environment is that of co-opting the post-conflict stakeholders towards U.S. policy objectives. Nye argues that this soft power rests on the ability to shape the preferences of other and co-opt rather than coerce.[41] The post conflict period is the pivotal period that must rely on shaping preferences to achieve mutual outcomes. This transfer effects what military planners call the center of gravity analysis. The center of gravity has radically changed in the post conflict stage driving the need to change the approach.

In U.S. Army doctrine, the analysis of the center of gravity assist in identifying elements in which to better pursue desired objectives. In conventional military operations the center of gravity analysis concentrates on defeated an opposing force or an element that challenges the pursuit of strategic end states. In the transition phasing between the conflict period and the stability and reconstruction phase, these centers of gravity essentially transform from an enemy to that of other elements that prevent the achievement of policy objectives. The center of gravity analysis for the conventional phase of intervention is no longer valid. A new center of gravity analysis is therefore required that incorporates an understanding of the evolved influences of power and the new environment.

---

[40]Nye, *The Future of Power*, 10.

[41]Joseph S. Nye Jr., *Soft Power: the Means to Success in World Politics* (New York: Public Affairs, 2005), 5-6. Nye first introduced this concept in *Bound to Lead: The Changing Nature of American Power* (New York: Basic Books, 1990), chapter 2.

In his discussion on the components of power, Nye utilizes three aspects of relational power. He characterizes these three aspects of relational power as the "faces of power". The faces of power are commanding change, controlling agendas and establishing preferences. The first face utilizes coercion or rewards to change behavior overtly. The second face of power controls the agenda of actions to limit options and the third face of power creates and shapes beliefs, perceptions and preferences to promote desired outcomes.[42]

In the conventional conflict phase, the first face of power overtly compels compliance. The threat or use of force by military power achieves the desire outcome of the neutralization of an element that is preventing progress towards the policy objectives of state intervention. However, once the military force is defeated the requirement to review and implement any of the three aspects of relational power is necessary. The ability to discern elements of power from a population or nation state emerging from conflict is ripe with either challenges or opportunities. There is even support for the argument that the transition period may have a preferential avenue of power expression that offers a more effective progression towards a stable and legitimate end state far from that of coercion. "Years of research suggest that empathy and social intelligence are vastly more important to acquiring and exercising power than are force, deception, or terror."[43]

In summary, the use of military force is one of many elements of power in the immediate post war period. It is not however the only resource available to the U.S. in pursuing policy objectives following conflict operations. The complexity and dynamics of the twenty-first century have evolved the nineteenth-century definition of a "great power" as that which prevails in war.[44] The attempt at leveraging optimal solutions in translating military victories into foreign policy

---

[42]Robert A. Dahl, *Who Governs: Democracy and Power in an American City* (New Haven, CT: Yale University Press, 1961). Synapsis extracted from Nye, *The Future of Power*, 10-19.

[43]Keltner, Dacher, "The Power Paradox," *Greater Good* (Winter 2007-2008), 15.

[44]Nye, *The Future of Power*, 4–5.

achievements utilizing one source of national power is unwise. Policy leaders, such as Secretary of Defense Robert Gates, have voiced this concern over the comprehensive application of state power in future endeavors. "I am here to make the case for strengthening our capacity to use soft power and for better integrating it with hard power."[45] The development and implementation of one individual index of power is doomed to fail because power is contingent upon human relationships that vary in different cultures and contexts.[46] This is a certainty in the transition period.

Cultural Considerations and Narrative

Culture is the distinct ways that different societies express values, norms and behavior in their daily lives. It is "shared set of traditions, belief systems and behaviors."[47] It is an integral element to how societies will respond and behave in the transition period. Understanding and utilization of conceptual models of culture can assist in enabling a more holistic approach in transition planning. The lack of a cultural understanding in the environment can lead to an increase in animosity and opposition by elements of the society as well as the inadvertent contributions to counterproductive spoilers preventing progress towards stability.

Culture and the decision making power are invariably linked. How the culture or societal elements influence the transitional period will be contingent upon the contextual and historical structures of that nation. Sociologist Steven Lukes believes that these ideas and beliefs assist in shaping initial preferences in individuals and populations.[48] In what Lukes describes as "The

---

[45]Thom Shanker, "Defense Secretary Urges More Spending for U.S. Diplomacy," *New York Times* (27 November 2007).

[46]Nye, *The Future of Power*, 9-10.

[47]William D. Wunderle, *Through the Lens of Cultural Awareness* (New York: BiblioGov, 2012), 3.

[48]Steven Lukes, *Power: A Radical View*, 2nd ed. (London: Palgrave Macmillian, 2005), 15.

Third Dimension of Power" these beliefs influence decision making in both overt and covert ways. This ideological expression of power influences the desires of a population, even if those overt desires are opposed to their individual self-interest.[49] The understanding of the core cultural concepts within the society can contribute to leveraging disparate interests in a post conflict environment. This approach may assist in integrating "spoilers" in the transitional period towards agreed upon and accepted end states. One methodology towards a better understanding the societal dynamics is the cultural conceptual model.

Cultural models can additionally assist external actors in developing approaches that not only serve to integrate regional players but leverage the most effective means in which to set conditions for stability efforts. Social scientist Carl Solberg offers a model that assists in understanding culture and its influencing manifestations. It consists of cultural influences, dimensions (variations) and manifestations.[50]

The first component is that of cultural influences. Heritage, religion, language and traditions are the elements that bind cultures together. The collective perception of the past by the society defines the culture's ethnic and national identity. While the influences are not absolute, the tendencies of culture shape the way people think and behave. These considerations can assist in the structuring of planning and transitional governmental institutions in the post conflict period and determine what range of change is culturally acceptable to the society.[51] National identity and heritage coupled with these cultural influences are components of resiliency within the society. This resiliency of the society promotes coping mechanisms in adjusting to the transition environment.

---

[49]Ibid., 25.

[50]Carl Arthur Solberg, *Culture and Industrial Buyer Behavior: The Arab Experience* (Dijon, France, September 2002), 5.

[51]Wunderle, *Through the Lens of Cultural Awareness*, 12. Subcomponents of cultural influences include: History and Foreign Heritage, Social Organization, Traditions and Language.

The second component includes cultural variations. The styles of behavior and values held by a society formulate ways of thinking and preferences. Social rules, cultural structures and symbols all contribute to the social variation of a particular culture. The integrative elements of communicating and interaction within the society pre and post transition shape the conditions for future cooperation.[52]

The last component in this model consists of cultural manifestations. How the culture displays behavior through perceptions of authority, compromise, risk and negotiating style will largely affect the behavior of many elements in the post conflict society. The understanding of the interacting variables within the population and its representatives offers better insight in the initial interactions with regional stakeholders.[53] By responding to unusual expressions of cultural manifestations without the understanding of the influences and variations that created them, the transition and future stability efforts may become more difficult.

The Solberg cultural conceptual model is a targeted approach at enabling resiliency of populations under stress. In the manuscript, *Human Security: A Framework for Assessment in Conflict and Transition*, Dr. Jennifer Leaning argues that a narrow focus on material resources has prevented analysts from identifying the true sources of vulnerability or resilience in a population. The resiliency of a community relies on how well their core attachments of home, community and the future remain intact. A "core bundle" of resources -material, psychological and social- that address minimum human survival requirements provide the floor from which development efforts can then push off. If the basic core requirements are not guaranteed,

---

[52]Ibid., 13–17. Subcomponents include Behaviors (Context Sensitivity), Values (Individualism vs. Collectivism, Power Distance, Formality vs. informality, Uncertainty Avoidance and Long-term vs Short Term orientation) and Cognition (Reasoning Styles).

[53]Ibid., 18.

development gains will be short lived.[54] By focusing more directly on the individuals and their culture in context of the conflict, planner can better assess measures to mitigate conflict escalation. This approach can assist planners in developing options that build upon core resiliency in post conflict populations.

The human security approach is useful in an unfamiliar or evolved environment. Its components reflect not only the need for basic human survival but also the elements to sustain and develop a core coping capacity in general populations under stress. The two main components being: 1) how to secure minimum levels of survival (water, food, shelter) and minimum levels of protection and 2) how to support basic psychosocial needs to support identity, recognition, participation and autonomy. These elements provide an essential base for human development. By ensuring this base is in place for any given population, there are immediate benefits in population threat management and social efficacy. Minimal levels of societal functionality are therefore the initial requirements in long-term stability efforts. Human security and its basal components for survival must be attained prior to and as a pre-condition for the effective implantation of long-term reconstruction and nation state enabling.[55]

While established government in society regulates cultural behavior to some extent, the twenty first century has witness a diffusion of power towards non-state actors. The relevant power of societies and their people has more influence in shaping the post conflict environment. This influence and the ability to share information have created a new environment where it is no longer effective to attempt to establish control over populations. It has become necessary to set and pursue objectives and end states with collaborative goals. An understanding of culture and

---

[54]Jennifer Leaning and Sam Arie, "Human Security: A Framework for Assessment in Conflict and Transition," *Tulane University/CERTI initiative* (December 2010), 4.

[55]Leaning, "Human Security: A Framework for Assessment in Conflict and Transition," 12.

values that a population holds in high regard and how these values can contribute to shared end states is necessary to implement effective transitional measures.

The environment created by high intensity combat operations is inherently a fractious one. Populations within the nation experience dislocation, infrastructure collapse, resource shortages and even collateral effects. The security transitional gap following conventional warfare changes the dynamics of a new environment that demands a culturally grounded approach that incorporates all stakeholders progressing towards a defined end state. The effective holistic approach reinforces existing cultural ideals of the society. This includes an understanding of the strategic cultures and agendas of both friend and foe.[56]

The effective union of the holistic approach and stability confidence building is to incorporate positive and limit negative constructs of a population's local power and ownership schemas. Robert Rubinstein and Diane Keller suggest addressing seven principles to achieve societal based stability. The seven principles to consider concerning culture and conflict transition are: 1) understanding meaning and interacting with the culture in a culturally positive manner, 2) awareness of cultural symbols, 3) avoiding assumptions that all local nationals share the same motives, 4) differences in local conflict management practices, 5) the emphasis on ensuring mutual expectations are understood by local nationals and interventionist actors, 6) avoiding displays or actions of preference towards any one social group and finally, 7) an understanding of the cultural hierarchies of power, influence and expertise.[57] These principles can assist in the development of a range of options that promote rather than undermine the inherent social stability mechanisms.

---

[56]Ibid., 7.

[57]Robert A. Rubinstein, Diana M. Keller and Michael E. Scherger, "Culture and interoperability in integrated Missions," *International Peacekeeping* 15, no.4 (2008): 540–555.

In summary, the transitional challenge remains one of correctly framing the cultural and contextual environment and identifying the positive or negative elements that will influence the transition. High levels of human capital, a centralized secular government and a westernized heritage enabled the reconstruction efforts in Germany following the Second World War. Conversely, nations such as Somalia and Afghanistan's historical lack of legitimate rule of law systems, factionalized power bases and weak national identities created challenges to establishing a stable environment for long-term stability. "As a first step in any game, it helps to start by figuring out who is holding the high cards and how many chips that player has. Equally important, however, is that policy makers have the contextual intelligence to understand what game they are playing."[58] The ability to convey and convert resources into realized power within the transition period to obtain desired outcomes requires well-planned strategies implemented by knowledgeable implementers. With a more comprehensive and holistic approach planners are more able to deal with the complexities of transitioning from a conflict environment towards a more stable one.

Conceptual Planning Approaches

The transition point between conflict and peacekeeping operations is the bridge in achieving overall policy objectives. These policy objectives or grand strategies are the unifying linkages encompassing the conflict and stability phases. As nation states must act purposefully over time, grand strategies are the overall plans for how states can capitalize on the political, economic, and military means employed to achieve their stated objectives.[59] The use of conceptual planning approaches may assist in complementing established planning while

---

[58]Nye, *The Future of Power*, 11.

[59]Richard Samuels, *Securing Japan: Tokyo's Grand Strategy and the Future of East Asia* (Ithaca: Cornell, 2007), 1–6.

maintaining the linkage to policy. They additionally provide the flexibility in which to adapt or reorient efforts based on conceptual points linking policy and preferred end states. The inability of systematic approaches in Iraq and Afghanistan towards achieving policy objectives emphasized the critical need to incorporate supplementary cognitive frameworks that existing planning did not address.[60]

The military community looked towards theoretical models in the social sciences and the scientific method to provide insight in overcoming the complex challenges presented by post conflict operations. The introduction of the Army Design Methodology (ADM) approach has opened the possibility for a broad utilization of conceptual and cognitive approaches in addressing the post conflict period. Army doctrine recognizes that there consists of two separate complementary components of planning. The formal processes of detailed planning such the Military Decision Making Process (MDMP) or the Joint Operations Planning Process (JOPP) are one component. The supporting and complementary component of Design is the second. Army doctrine describes Design as "not a function to be accomplished, but rather a living process. Is should reflect ongoing learning and adaptation."[61] In a post conflict environment that entails a great deal of complexity this flexible approach allows conceptual frameworks to provide continuous assessments and reframing to support concurrent planning. Design supports this by emphasizing, "a methodology for applying critical and creative thinking to understand, visualize, and describe complex, ill-structured problems and develop approaches to solve them."[62] The question is then what conceptual tools can support and best assist in the post conflict period.

---

[60]Stefan J. Banach, "Educating By Design: Preparing Leaders for a Complex World," *Military Review* March-April (2009), 97.

[61]U.S. Army, United States Army Field Manual (FM) 3–24 *Counterinsurgency* (Washington, DC: Government Printing Office, 2006), 4–28.

[62]U.S. Army, United States Army Field Manual (FM) 5–0, *The Operations Process* (Washington, DC: Government Printing Office, 2010), 3–1.

The post conflict environment challenges linear planning and structured problem framing. The unpredictable and dynamic elements of political, social, cultural and military factors and their interrelationships often resist a comprehensive understanding and straightforward solution for commanders. The ADM leverages critical thinking and innovation within a framework of collaboration that enables understanding of the environment, establishing the correct problem set, and developing operational approaches. It provides a conceptual building block that attempts to incorporate multiple perspectives. In the ADM, one may consider options separate from conventional linear planning and incorporate more holistic approaches that align with operational and strategic objectives. ADM is a creative and non-linear framework utilizing a wide range of different processes applicable to any particular problem or environment. It borrows from a diverse range of academic fields such as organizational theory, general systems theory and complexity theory in offering holistic management of complex problems. Using theoretical models and cognitive tools commanders and planners can correctly frame the problem and discern operational approaches. The use of the systems thinking approach is one of the available tools in understanding the complexity of the transition period.

The ADM provides the cognitive space to appreciate this complex environment by leveraging systems thinking to understand the transition period. The transition to the post conflict environment is not solely the termination of kinetic military operations but a pattern of change with underlying structures. "Systems thinking is a discipline for seeing wholes. It is a framework for seeing interrelationships rather than things, for seeing pattern of change rather than static snapshots."[63] Organizational theorist, Peter Senge, promotes the idea of using 'system archetypes' as a systems model that describes the causality and reinforcing feedback inherent to

---

[63]Peter M. Senge, *The Fifth Discipline: the Art and Practice of the Learning Organization*, rev. ed. (New York: Doubleday, 2006), 68.

34

many complex situations. These 'circles of causality' reveal feedback and relational mechanisms that linear approaches may not divulge.[64]

System models and theory can be helpful in developing a conceptual planning approach and implementation in this time constrained post conflict evolved environment. In the book, *The Fifth Discipline*, author Peter Senge outlines archetypes to generic systems that exhibit reoccurring patterns based on their systems structure. These system archetypes can assist planners and stakeholders in discerning relatively simple elements underlying the complexity of interrelated systems.[65] One of his system archetypes is the Escalation Model. This model focuses on the relative advantages of competing organizations. Conflict and post conflict environments are the product of competing systems or organizations. The alleviation of the causal factors of conflict and the promotion of integrating interest would theoretically establish favorable conditions in the transition phase and support longer-term stability interests.

The Escalation Model draws from the theory that two or more factions perceive their well-being as dependent on a relative advantage to an opposing organization.[66] Increased advantage by one faction increases the perceived threat of the other, which in turn increases the overall level of instability and aggression. Perceptions, real or otherwise, further promote this increasing level of counterproductive reactions as defensive mechanisms serve to protect the organizational self-interest. The transition period following conflict is a timeframe in which stakeholders undergo power realignment. This may lead to increased violence and affect institution building that is dependent upon time and a stable environment. According to Senge,

---

[64]Ibid., 93. As cited by Senge, researchers have identified over a dozen of system archetypes. He presents nine in the cited reference. All archetypes consist of the system building blocks of reinforcing processes, balancing processes and delays.

[65]Ibid., 93.

[66]Ibid., 395. This model is outlined in Appendix 2 along with other system models that conform to relational and feedback criteria.

the management principle to alleviate this cycle of counterproductive actions is explore options or planning avenues that promote the achievement of a factions objectives. Often this takes the form of "aggressive peaceful" actions by external actors or opposing factions in deescalating this cycle.

Various system archetypes address different influences in a complex system thinking literature. Senge's model is just one example of a possible way planners can reassess the evolved post conflict environment in a time-constrained circumstance. Transition and the post conflict environment is a dynamic system. This system will evolve into the stability phase or regress to conflict based on the measures implemented by the various stakeholders. The systems approach and its appreciation for understanding complexity can offer stakeholders methods to pursue integrated and agreed upon strategies to overall productive end states.

The transition from conflict illustrates a complex and ill-structured problem set. Operational problems are often defined as well structured, medium structured and ill-structured.[67] Ill-structured or complex problem sets involving multi layered dynamic systems or societal interactions require a developed understanding to facilitate operational planning. In the post conflict transition, this utilization of a systems approach in reevaluating the environment may be necessary due to the distinct and defining change in contextual dynamics in a short time frame. The effects of conflict and evolving power, cultural and social structures have undergone a relatively rapid system change. Operation reframing is necessary to appreciate the evolved environment. Previous planning efforts and prioritization however detailed, may not have addressed critically defining aspects of this post conflict context.

The chapter has examined ways in which to build upon cognitive concepts that may assist in the integration of efforts in the transition. The non-material influences discussed in the previous chapter are by definition complex and dynamic elements. The relationships of power

---

[67]U.S. Army, TP 525-5-500 *Commander's Appreciation and Campaign Design* (Fort Monroe, VA: US Army Training and Doctrine Command, 28 January 2008), 8-11.

and cultural contribute to this complexity. This complexity continues to expand as the post conflict environment evolves and systems respond to each other. Operational planners and interested stakeholders must incorporate a wide range of information and then apply measures rapidly in an evolved and still changing transitional environment. An understanding of the transition environment utilizing a system thinking approach can reveal opportunities within the post conflict period. These opportunities could complement the existing planning for the transition period and optimally incorporate a wider range of stability stakeholders.

Historical Variances

Nation building and post conflict transition are not a new challenge for the U.S. and the international community. Interventions in the Philippines, Germany, Italy, Japan, South Korea, Panama and Kuwait are historical examples of post conflict nations that have overcome the challenges of post conflict instability and established enduring institutions.[68] The nations of Iraq and Afghanistan are currently still dealing with the effects of conflict and continue to pursue long-term enduring stability.[69] The lessons of previous post conflict situations offer insight to specific contexts. However, they are not necessarily the universal solution in future state interventions. Nevertheless, the lessons provide a basis for discussion to the complex problem set of the transition period. A brief review of these interventions will reveal the range of variance in the post conflict evolution.

Post conflict planning in the Panamanian conflict was incomplete during the transition from kinetic operations. Commanders complained of vague guidance on implementing stability

---

[68]Lieutenant Colonel Brian De Toy, ed., *Turning Victory into Success. Military Operations after the Campaign*, 1st ed. (Fort Leavenworth, KS: Combat Studies Institute Press, 2004), 2.

[69]Ibid., 3.

measures and a lack of specialized personnel qualified in stability operations.[70] As decisive offensive operations concluded, the environment quickly and unexpectedly evolved into chaos. U.S. forces were unprepared for the ensuing security vacuum that came about following the surrender of the Panamanian defense force. As to whether it was the adaptability of the ground forces or the subsequent efforts of the emergent government towards establishing order remains unclear.[71] Since the Panamanian intervention, the government has peacefully transitioned political power from a range of diverse parties and currently ranks as one of the top three Central American nations in human development programs.[72]

In the Haiti intervention, the long crisis period and lessons imported from the Panama and Somalia experiences facilitated detailed post conflict planning. Operation Uphold Democracy experienced increased interagency cooperation and detailed planning criteria. The "Interagency Checklist for Restoration of Essential Services" included such considerations as reestablishing civic administration, elections, information services, law enforcement rebuilding, and refugee control and disaster preparedness.[73] However, despite this detailed planning the post conflict period transitioned to a long period of social and political instability that has yet to be fully resolved.

In the first gulf war during Operation Desert Storm commanders complained of the lack of trained personnel and a post conflict plan to stabilize and reconstruct Kuwait following the

---

[70]John T. Fishel, *The Fog of Peace: Planning and Executing the Restoration of Panama* (Carlisle Barracks, PA: USAWC Strategic Studies Institute, April 1992), 32-44.

[71]Lieutenant Colonel John Fishel and Major Richard Downie, "Taking Responsibility for Our Actions? Establishing Order and Stability in Panama," *Military Review* (April 1992): 63.

[72]UNDP Human Development Report 2010, http://hdr.undp.org/en/media/HDR_2010_EN_Complete.pdf. (accessed on 4 February, 2013), 144.

[73]Conrad C. Crane, *Landpower and Crises: Army Roles and Missions in Smaller-Scale Contingencies During the 1990s* (Carlisle,PA: Strategic Studies Institute, U.S. Army War College, January 2001), 20.

cessation of combat operations. Only the improvisation of Army engineers and civil affairs personnel enabled the eventual success of the post war effort in setting the conditions for long-term stability.[74] At present time, Kuwait continues to be a center of stability and economic growth for the region.

These historical variances highlight that each intervention raises unique contextual challenges that lead to a range of enduring end states. In Panama, due to cultural influences that played out in the post conflict period, the social and civic environment mitigated the lack of detailed planning and stability efforts progressed. In Haiti, despite the detailed planning and interagency cooperation, the environmental influences proved resistant to enduring stability efforts. The overall lesson learned in the post-conflict transition is that lessons learned from the last intervention are not necessarily applicable to the next. An appreciation of transitional influences and the systems thinking approach can provide the operational frame in which to incorporate the unique elements of the specific situational context without treating the transitional period as a generic problem with universal solutions. The case studies of Iraq and Panama will reveal specific areas that will serve to highlight the need for a holistic appreciation of the contextual transitional problem to enable stakeholders to prepare for the post conflict period.

CASE STUDY: IRAQ

In 2003, the U.S. government declared that the Iraqi regime was an imminent threat to regional and global security. The American and British governments solidified a coalition of 40 nations and committed ground forces on 20 March 2003. By 9 May, the coalition forces had

---

[74]Janet A. McDonnell, *After Desert Storm: The U.S. Army and the Reconstruction of Kuwait* (Washington, DC: Government Printing Office, 1999), 32.

decisively defeated the Iraqi military and the Saddam regime collapsed. American internal involvement in Iraq would continue until officially concluded on 15 December 2011.[75]

On 1 May 2003, President George Bush declared that major combat operations had ended and the Coalition was now engaged in securing and stability efforts in Iraq.[76] Localized security efforts focused on small-scale instability pockets and the pursuit of Ba'athist regime leaders that had gone in hiding. The post conflict transitional phase gradually evolved into a growing insurgency. The insurgent Ramadan offensive, consisting of wide spread insurgent attacks against Coalition targets, in October of 2003 signaled the beginning of a long-term effort to return stability to Iraq. The post-conflict transition had passed and counter insurgency would consume international efforts and span nearly nine years.

In mid-April of 2003, the post transitional security gap had materialized. Conventional operations had concluded, but the stability efforts that characterize Phase IV operations had yet to mature. Coalition military efforts had dismantled the conventional Iraqi forces and the Saddam Hussein governmental regime. Six months would pass before the Ramadan Offensive would definitely declare the post conflict transition concluded. The pre-conflict planning and post-conflict implementation did not establish the conditions for long-term stability. These outcomes are in part attributable to the fact that efforts during the transitional period did not produce the conditions for enduring stability.

This analysis consists of three sections. First, it will look at the lack of a common understanding of the transition period. Second, it will review the inability to integrate efforts of the stakeholders at the coalition level and then subsequently the Iraqi state and regional levels.

---

[75]U.S. Department of Defense News, "Dempsey: Iraq Campaign Was worth the Cost" (15 December 2011): 1, http://www.defense.gov/news/newsarticle.aspx?id=66488 (accessed 4 February 2013).

[76]CBS News Archive, "Text of Bush Speech," CBS News, May 1, 2003, 3. http://www.cbsnews.com/2100-500257_162-551946.html (accessed February 4, 2013).

Third, it will evaluate the understanding of the elements of culture and power following the fall of the Ba'athist regime.

Understanding of the Transition Gap

COBRA II was the CFLCC (Combined Forces Land Component Command) operations plan for the invasion of Iraq. COBRA II encompassed all the phases of the military campaign to include the Phase IV or stability portion. Primary staff planners identified the need to detail the Phase IV portion of the plan as early as January of 2003. Initial planning assumptions for the Phase IV included the Coalition's ability to recall the Iraqi Army and bureaucracy to assist in reconstruction. The initial policy guidance from Washington was that the removal of Ba'athist regime leadership would target only the highest levels of government. [77] The initial efforts of the CFLCC planners focused on establishing localized security and ensuring the mitigation of population distress through humanitarian assistance enabling.

As the cessation of major conventional operations approached, military planners continued to update ongoing assessments as the post conflict period materialized. The planners further identified a developing operational requirement that would have to address the emerging complexities of the post conflict period.[78] ECLIPISE II was the name of the planning sequel that reframed the operational scope of the Phase IV phase. Figure 4 outlines the operational framing of the post conflict environment as outlined by the CFLCC planners.

---

[77]Kevin Benson, "Phase IV: A Planner's Reply to Brigadier General Alywin-Foster," *Military Review* (March-April 2006): 62.

[78]US Army Training and Doctrine Command/CSI 2004 Conference Papers, *Turning Victory Into Success: Two Centuries of American Campaigning* (Fort Leavenworth, KS: CSI Press, 204), 184.

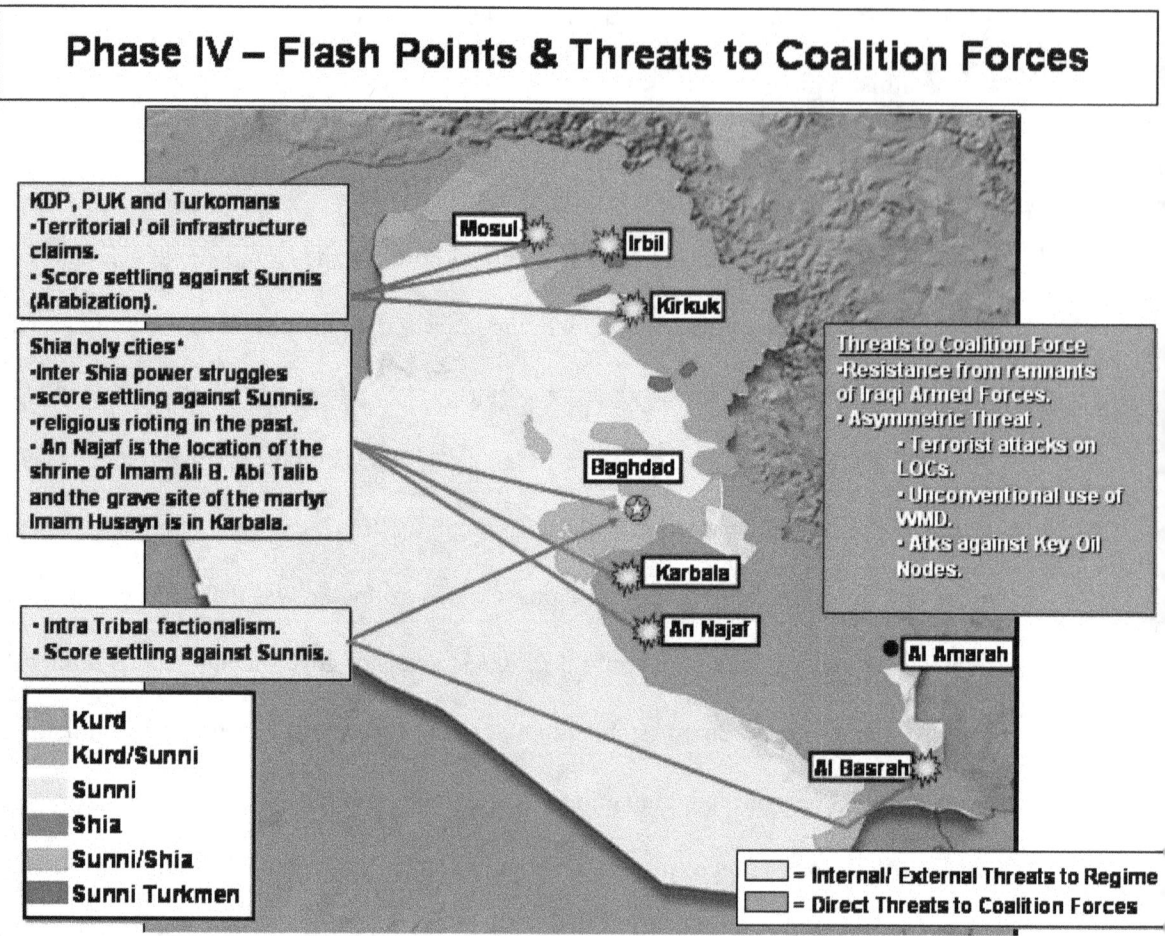

Phase IV – Flash Points & Threats to Coalition Forces

KDP, PUK and Turkomans
-Territorial / oil infrastructure claims.
- Score settling against Sunnis (Arabization).

Shia holy cities*
-Inter Shia power struggles
-score settling against Sunnis.
-religious rioting in the past.
- An Najaf is the location of the shrine of Imam Ali B. Abi Talib and the grave site of the martyr Imam Husayn is in Karbala.

- Intra Tribal factionalism.
- Score settling against Sunnis.

Threats to Coalition Force
-Resistance from remnants of Iraqi Armed Forces.
- Asymmetric Threat.
    - Terrorist attacks on LOCs.
    - Unconventional use of WMD.
    - Atks against Key Oil Nodes.

Mosul
Irbil
Kirkuk
Baghdad
Karbala
An Najaf
Al Amarah
Al Basrah

Kurd
Kurd/Sunni
Sunni
Shia
Sunni/Shia
Sunni Turkmen

= Internal/ External Threats to Regime
= Direct Threats to Coalition Forces

Figure 2. Updated Phase IV Environment Iraq

Source: US Army Training and Doctrine Command/CSI 2004 Conference Papers

CFLCC planners continued to reassess and update estimates for the post conflict period appreciating the temporal gap that would follow cessation of conventional operations. This critical period highlighted the necessary contextual importance of the initial actions necessary for setting the conditions for future stability efforts. However, the decisions of May and June of 2003 to transform CFLCC responsibility to the V CORPS were to challenge the effective implementation of transitional operations. In 15 June 2003, the responsibility for the continued progress of Phase IV transferred to V CORP with the criteria outlined in Figure 3.

CFLCC ENDSTATE CONDITIONS

Lines of Operation	Handover Conditions
ACHIEVE IRAQI, REGIONAL AND INTERNATIONAL SUPPORT – Integrate and leverage Coalition efforts to establish a secure and stable environment within a self sufficient Iraqi nation.	• The Iraqi people tolerate the interim administration. • Neighboring countries do not actively oppose the Coalition effort to establish a new Iraqi government.
SECURITY Establish a secure and stable environment for CFLCC transition to CJTF-7.	• Pockets of organized resistance are defeated. • Territorial integrity of Iraq is intact. • SSE operations transitioned to follow on forces. • Security is established for LOGCAP personnel. • Initiate use of Iraqi military for stability operations. • Establish confinement facility inside Iraq
RULE OF LAW – Exercise control through the existing legal system and operate in accordance with international law.	• Civil order is maintained • Functioning police force exist
INFRASTRUCTURE RECOVERY Initiate restoration of Iraqi self-sufficiency.	• Repairs of damaged essential civil and economic infrastructure are underway.
HUMANITARIAN RELIEF AND ASSISTANCE - Mitigate human suffering.	• Emergency HA is provided by the civilian sector and IOs/NGOs. • Support is provided to IO/NGO for Sustainment HA.
GOVERNANCE AND ADMINISTRATION Exercise military authority.	• Temporary military authority is established at National level and in all 18 provinces.

Figure 3. CFLCC Handover Criteria

Source: US Army Training and Doctrine Command/CSI 2004 Conference Papers

The U.S. military planning for the post conflict environment was proactive and entailed an appreciation for the transition period. However, this execution of planning, while arguably optimistic in its projected goals, suffered a series of disconnects. Notably the previous planning assumptions of recalling the Iraqi Army and the leveraging of the mid-to-lower level Ba'athist in reestablishing order and governance were to prove untrue. Senior military and policy levels continued to modify U.S. structures and policy goals during a period of time that necessitated unified post conflict stability measures.[79] This significantly affected the ability of previous planning estimates to readjust to the new policy directives. The change in policy directives in the summer of 2003 nullified the planning assumptions that intended to alleviate the instable transitional effects. While the CFLCC planners exhibited a developed understanding of the transition period, the limited ability to reorient in the transition period was not enough to fill the societal and established governmental vacuum. The capability of operational military ground forces in reacting, reassessing and implementing localized stability enhancing measures proved unable to curtail a societal descent into an insurgent environment.

The supporting civilian agencies of the U.S. government were less appreciative and prepared for the transition period. The majority of the governmental structures of the Iraqi central and local governments had collapsed when the Office for Reconstruction and Humanitarian Assistance (ORHA) and its successor, the Coalition Provisional Authority (CPA), began administration efforts in April and May of 2003.[80] The Iraqi security institutions dissolved rapidly in the weeks and months following the cessation of major conflict. The absence of the established governmental and security institutions opened the door to widespread disorder that heightened instability levels throughout the country. The commander of the US Army's V Corps, Lieutenant-General William Wallace was to later comment that: "What in fact happened, which was unanticipated at least in [my mind], is that when [we] decapitated the regime, everything below it fell apart."[81] As the ORHA and later the CPA began to initiate planning and implementation of

---

[79]Thomas E. Ricks, *Fiasco: The American Military Adventure in Iraq, 2003 to 2005*, reprint (New York: Penguin Books, 2007), 145.

[80]Seth G. Jones, *Establishing Law and Order After Conflict* (Santa Monica, CA: Rand Publishing, 2005), 111.

[81]Interview with Lieutenant-General William Scott Wallace for *Frontline: invasion of Iraq*, available at http://www.pbs.org/wgbh/pages/frontline/shows/invasion/interviews/wallace.html (accessed 13 January 2013). See also Murray Williamson and Major General Robert

governmental reforms, the Coalition agencies began to experience a widening, 'security gap' and violence and instability levels began to rise. The dedicated efforts to open a dialogue with the newly established Iraqi Governing Council and implement a coordinated and integrated approach to the reconstruction of the Iraqi security sector was not realized until the end of 2003.[82] The governmental enabling efforts would continue to implement stability confidence measures; however, the transition period had passed and a new environment had evolved.

The post conflict period is susceptible to a wide range of influences that can modify existing planning constructs. A significant change in intervention policy during the transition period is one example. The U.S. military and its Coalition allies conducted extensive planning for the post conflict transitional period. This planning consisted of a detailed appreciation of the pivotal point in the post conflict environment. However, the overly focused security operations and humanitarian relief relied on the assumptions that the civic institutions of Iraq would maintain order and keep the government functioning following the collapse of the Ba'athist regime.[83] The supporting civilian agencies were unable to assist in mitigating these governmental shortfalls due to varying issues. Predominantly the appreciation of the post conflict period and the necessity to incorporate tailored and swift response to set favorable conditions was lacking. The U.S. civilian agencies were unable to implement rapid measures of administration to alleviate rising instability. Coupled with the institutional incapability of the Iraqi populace to enact effective and relative governmental reforms, the environment evolved from post conflict transition to larger scale insurgency, lasting nearly nine years.

H. Scales, Jr., *The Iraq War: A Military History* (Cambridge, MA: Belknap Press of Harvard University Press, 2003) for a more detailed review.

[82] Jones, *Establishing Law and Order after Conflict*, 116.

[83] James Fallows, "Blind into Baghdad," *The Atlantic Monthly* (January/February 2004): 3.

<u>Stakeholder Integration</u>

The inability of the Coalition stakeholders to integrate planning for the post conflict environment further limited the ability to incorporate Iraqi national and regional actors in the transition process. The U.S. Central Command (USCENTCOM) original plan for Phase IV operations detailed military supported stability operations for up to eighteen months. The original Phase IV planning, while detailed, did not proceed as intended due to an evolution of events leading up to the transition period. One of the primary CFLCC planners, Colonel Kevin Benson highlighted some of the challenges of rapidly implementing unified operations in the evolving transition period.

> The challenge was translating the plans into action while dealing with guidance and assumptions from higher echelons of command, the deployment process, and evolving policy. As a result, our plans never quite evolved to link ground operations to logical lines of operation that would lead to setting solid military conditions for policy objectives. [84]

The Office of Reconstruction and Humanitarian Agency (ORHA), established two months prior to the ground invasion, was the DOD supported agency to lead the post conflict transition. According to General Tommy Franks, the coordination between USCENTCOM and ORHA was constant throughout the pre-invasion period. However, this constant coordination did not emphasize the integration of U.S. stakeholders but delineated it.

> My concern was prompted in part by America's recent warfighting history. During the Vietnam War, Defense Secretary Robert McNamara and his Whiz Kids had repeatedly picked individual bombing targets and approved battalion-sized maneuvers. That was not going to happen in Iraq. I knew the President and Don Rumsfeld would back me up, so I felt free to pass the message along to the bureaucracy beneath them: *You pay attention to the day* after and *I'll pay attention to the day* of (emphasis in original). [85]

---

[84]Kevin Benson, "Phase IV: A Planner's Reply to Brigadier General Alywin-Foster," 62.

[85]Tommy Franks and Malcolm McConnell, *American Soldier* (New York: Harper Collins, 2004), 441.

To be sure, there were localized efforts at integrating Coalition stakeholders in the planning process. Benson describes numerous attempts at incorporating civilian agencies and planners in the planning process during the conventional phase of the conflict. "Whitley and Colonel Marty Stanton, the head of CFLCC's C9 (civil-military operations cell), worked to get international agencies and the U.N. back into Iraq.[86] These and other efforts proved unable to fully integrate the interagency community and provide a workable framework for the transition period.

Perhaps the greatest example of the lack of integrated planning prior to the intervention was concerning prewar civilian agencies estimates for the post conflict period. The Department of State had created reconstruction estimates prior to the invasion outlined in *The Future of Iraq Project*. This project, begun in October of 2001, was the most comprehensive planning conducted by the State Department prior to the Iraqi invasion. This document contained a range of observations and recommendations for the initial considerations in restoring Iraq following the conflict. The effort was particularly noteworthy in that it assembled over 200 Iraqi exiles to analyze how Iraqi society, culture and political institutions could reform after the fall of the Saddam regime.[87] The project addressed the issue of de-Ba'athification and warned that lack of an integrating element towards reincorporating this sector of society may "present a destabilizing element, especially if they are left without work or ability to get work."[88]

---

[86]Benson, "Phase IV: A Planner's Reply to Brigadier General Alywin-Foster," 62.

[87]US Department of State, "White House Applauds Results of Iraqi Opposition Conference", press release, 17 Dec. 2002. http://war-in-iraq.diktaali.net/links/zip/U_S_%20Department%20of%20State%20-%20Future%20of%20Iraq.htm (accessed 12 November 2013).

[88]National Security Archive, "The Future of Iraq Project Report: Working Group Recommendations," November 2002, http:www.gwu.edu/~nsarchiv/NSAEBB/NSAEBB198/index.htm (accessed 14 March 2013), 3.

The Defense Department neither integrated nor implemented any of its considerations during planning process or the post conflict period. *The Future of Iraq Project* was a holistic and comprehensive range of considerations that incorporated a wide range of stakeholders collaborating on the long-term stability interests in post war Iraq. The *Future of Iraq Project* and its finding were to prove prescient in many areas of the post conflict Iraq environment. The lack of its implementation in the consideration of operational planning serves to highlight the realities in the attempts at institutional integration in the Iraqi conflict of 2003.

U.S. policy directives attempt to establish a collaborative and integrated structure among governmental partners and streamline both planning processes and operational execution. The historical review of the integrative elements of the U.S. agencies supporting the post conflict environment suggests this continues to be challenging. However, as the strategic and policy objectives of state intervention remain paramount in overall operational efforts, the integrating function of planning frameworks may be the best avenue. These planning frameworks, if agreed upon can provide the necessary platform to shared understanding towards policy directed outcomes. The continued emphasis on common interest conveyed and understood by the interagency community will continue to be important to the holistic approach at post conflict opportunities management.

Influence of Power and Culture.

The Iraqi revolution of 1958 led the way for a series of coups that eventually saw the Sunni minority consolidate power in the Iraqi government. The Kurdish and Shiite establishment experienced an increasing disenfranchisement in the Iraqi power structure and government. The second Ba'athist coup in 1968 consolidated power in the Sunni minority and Saddam Hussein acceded to the presidency and control of the Revolutionary Command Council (RCC). The Iraqi Kurdish and Shia citizens were manipulated using force and tribal conciliation. Over time these group experienced a disenfranchisement from the civic institutions of the state. The Sunni

Ba'athist party dominated the influence of power and the means to express it.

Noted Middle Eastern historian Toby Dodge describes the elements in which the

Ba'athist "shadow state" excised power and leveraged influence.

> [F]irst, the deployment of extreme levels organized violence by the state to dominate and shape society; second, the use of state resources – jobs, development aid, and patronage – to buy the loyalty of sections of society; third, the use of oil revenue by the state to increase its autonomy from society; and, finally, the exacerbation and re-creation by the state of communal and ethnic divisions as a strategy of rule. These interlinked problems have fueled the state's domestic illegitimacy; its tendency to embark on military adventurism beyond its own borders, and even the Baathist regime's drive to acquire weapons of mass destruction. Seen this perspective, Saddam Hussein must be understood less as the cause of Iraq's violent political culture – or even of Iraq's role as a source of regional instability – and more as the symptom, albeit an extremely consequential one, of deeper, long-term dynamics within Iraq's political sociology.[89]

Following the Gulf War of 1991, the Iraqi government employed over 21 percent of the

population. Additionally, over 40 percent of Iraqis were dependent upon governmental payments

with many more applying for approval prior to the intervention.[90] The Ba'athist regime staffed

the state institutions and incorporated the applicant information into security networks in order to

penetrate all levels of Iraqi society and increase dependence upon the central government.

"Applications to receive a ration card gave the government crucial information about every

household under its control."[91] This in turn had a contributing effect on the core civic institutional

system inherent to Iraq and its ability to reconstitute a legitimate government following the

collapse of the Ba'athist regime.

---

[89]Toby Dodge, *Inventing Iraq: the Failure of Nation Building and a History Denied* (New York: Columbia University Press, 2005), 169–170.

[90]United Nations, "*Report to the Secretary General on Humanitarian Needs in Iraq by a Mission Led by Sadruddin Aga Khan, Executive Delegate of the Secretary General,*" (New York:15 July, 1991). http://www.casi.org.uk/info/undocs/s22799.html (accessed 01 March 2013).

[91]Ibid., 160.

This was not a proper state because these informal and highly personalized networks undermine the creation of a legal-rational bureaucracy and have a flexibility and tenacity that make them very difficult to root out. Coalition forces run the danger of unconsciously bolstering the networks of the shadow state created by the regime they ousted.[92]

Coalition planners expecting a reformed Iraqi government to reestablish functionality may have profited from a more holistic approach in considering the elements of contextual power by the existing state. If the establish societal control mechanisms are compromised in the transitional period they must be knowledgably replaced by other institutional or societal mechanisms. In order to alleviate the absence of previous institutional systems, the holistic approach must consider alternative options such as cultural or societal supporting constructs. Alternatively, the developed understanding of the resiliency of societal culture may reveal the necessity that the interim government must be reinforced by the intervening nation until these institutions demonstrate the ability to govern.

The expectation that by removing the senior levels of leadership in the regime would facilitate a reformed government to step forward and facilitate governance would not materialize. The influences of power and the cultural and religious fabric of the Iraqi society would resist a shared stakeholder solution without structured support from the intervening nations. The Iraqi nation and its societal support structure were compromised and unable to reinstitute itself due to cultural and historical influence. The transitional support was apparently not sufficient during the transition process and an insurgency began to evolve, develop and ultimately express itself in the later months of 2003.

The lessons from the post conflict period of the Iraqi invasion should serve to inform policy makers and planners on the perils of inadequately approaching the post conflict period. The components of understanding the post conflict environment, the integration of effort and the

---

[92]Ibid., 161.

appreciation of the influence of power and culture are just part of the complexity of the transition environment. A dedicated and continuously updated assessment of the transition period is an effective approach at detailing action following cessation of conflict. However, as this case study reveals, the lack of unity in implementation and the possibility of policy shift holds the potential for previous planning estimates to be invalid. The CFLCC planners for Phase IV operations in Iraq continued to adapt planning for a complex and highly evolving transition environment. However, incorrect assumptions on the cultural and intuitional influences of power in Iraq led to a vacuum of governance that the Iraq populace was incapable or unwilling to fill. The U.S. civilian agencies, due in part to interagency institutional resistance inhibited their ability to forecast and mitigate the regression of the transition period into an insurgent environment. The administration efforts of the civilian agencies and the integration of Iraqi stakeholders failed to develop an effective and stability-enhancing environment in the post conflict period and it degraded to an insurgency that would last nearly nine years.

CASE STUDY: PANAMA

The U.S. involvement in Panama was the first major use of force in the aftermath of the Cold War. Operation Just Cause demonstrated that the U.S. military forces could rapidly employ military forces and decisively defeat conventional enemy forces. However, this rapid conventional victory quickly evolved into a post invasion crisis. Panamanian society experienced an unusually high level of violence and instability following the cessation of conventional operations, but eventually emerged from the conflict on a progressive path towards a legitimate government and stability. This case study will review conditions of the intervention that contributed to the post conflict crisis and how they influenced the transition gap. The analysis will focus on the integration by U.S. stakeholders, operational understanding of the transition period and finally the relationship of power and culture in the environment.

51

The road to war began with the seizure of power by General Manual Noriega in 1981, following the death of General-President Omar Torrijos. Noriega consolidated power in Panama and created a de facto dictatorship characterized by violence, graft and drug involvement with Latin American cartels. The U.S. government began to consider intervention following a series of events that included Noriega's dismissal of election outcomes, the abuse of American citizens in Panama and the killing of a U.S. Marine officer by Panamanian police. Noriega even went to the extent of challenging intervention by declaring war on the U.S. The U.S. Army's XVIII Airborne Corps executed Operation Just Cause and militarily intervened in the nation of Panama in December of 1989. The justification for the intervention was to safeguard the lives of Americans, to defend democracy in Panama, to combat drug trafficking, and to protect the integrity of the Panama Canal Torrijos—Carter Treaties.[93]

U.S. Military planning for use of force in Panama began in February of 1988.[94] The post conflict portion of the plan, titled Operation Promote Liberty (originally named Blind Logic) focused on civil-military supporting operations with a mission to establish "stable democratic and economic institutions in Panama."[95] Assigned missions and responsibilities for post-conflict operations were vague and did not account for the effects of the combat operations and the regime change to the population at large.[96]

---

[93]New York Times, "A Transcript of President Bush's Address on the Decision to Use Force, 21 December 1989," http://www.nytimes.com/1989/12/21/world/fighting-panama-president-transcript-bush-s-address-decision-use-force-panama.html (accessed on December 13, 2012).

[94]John T. Fishel, *The Fog of Peace: Planning and Executing the Restoration of Panama*, 7.

[95]United States Special Operations Command, Memorandum for Commander in Chief, U.S. Southern Command, ATTN: J3, Quarry Heights, Panama, *Subject: Organization of Nation Building Forces*, 1-2.

[96]Fishel, *The Fog of Peace: Planning and Executing the Restoration of Panama*, 29-43.

On 20 December 1989, President George Bush ordered the execution of Operation Just Cause. In just eight days (20–28 December 1989), a force of 26,000 U.S. soldiers decisively defeated the Panamanian defense force (PDF) and captured Manual Noriega on 3 January 1990. The following post conflict transition was less decisive and not without its issues. The rapid and successful military operation to defeat the PDF quickly gave way to an evolved set of problems as the post conflict transition descended into a chaotic environment of looting and vandalism of Panama's infrastructure and governmental institutions.[97] The U.S. intervention and military operations in Panama validated the recently developed conventional AirLand Battle Doctrine but highlighted the need for considerably more thought on the events following conventional conflict.[98]

Understanding of the Transition Gap

The lack of an appreciation for the transition from conflict to stability condition setting started with national policy guidance. In Operation Just Cause the lack of policy guidance on the intervention end state did not detail desired outcomes that would guide transitional operations. "The planning that began in 1988 was strictly contingency planning, it was operations planning, what the Army call OPLANS. It was not done at the campaign level; it was not done at the strategy level."[99] This lack of identification of the transitional phase would have second order effects as military planners would conduct planning and operations that paralleled this policy

---

[97]John Fishel and Richard Downie, "Taking Responsibility for Our Actions? Establishing Order and Stability in Panama," 69-70.

[98]Airland Battle Doctrine was incorporated in U.S. Army doctrine in 1982. It was outlined in U.S. Army Field Manual (FM) 100-5 (1982) and detailed the conduct of conventional operations in a non-linear battlefield emphasizing continuous operations in depth and close coordination between air and ground forces.

[99]Richard H. Shultz, Jr., *In the Aftermath of War: U.S. Support for Reconstruction and Nation-Building in Panama Following Just Cause* (Maxwell AFB, AL: Air University Press, 1993), 17.

emphasis. The inability of military planners to account for the effects of the post conflict period and unforeseen destabilizing events would be the result. The intervention in Panama reveals the need for national policy guidance and policy guided end states to set the minimal conditions to progress from the conflict period.

In addition to the policy level issues in transition planning, the military operational planning failed to appreciate this post conflict period in several areas. One was the separation of the planning effort into two independent operational lines of planning effort by military command authorities. The second was the shortsightedness of military planners to organizationally structure forces for the post conflict phase. Finally, the failure to integrate civilian assistance, both in the interagency community and the local populace degraded the ability of the military in initially establishing transitional stability conditions.

The separation of the planning efforts created problems for setting stability conditions in the post conflict period. The initial planning lead for the post conflict portion fell under the responsibility of a small cell of U.S. Army Reserve officers from the J5 civil affairs section. Operation Blind Logic (renamed Operation Promote Liberty) was the post conflict contingency plan and fell under a different joint directorate. The planning and synchronization of Blind Logic with the operational plan suffered from compartmentalization and priority, up until the time of operational execution.[100] The two plans executed separately without a consideration of the transitional phase or condition setting for stability efforts. "What largely saved the situation in Panama and limited the damage to the security situation…was the existence of Blind Logic as

---

[100]US Army Training and Doctrine Command/CSI 2004 Conference Papers, *Turning Victory Into Success: Two Centuries of American Campaigning* (Fort Leavenworth, KS: CSI Press, 204), 170-173. See also John T. Fishel, Civil Military Operations in the New World (Westport, CT: Praeger Publisher, 1997), 33.

plan."[101] The base planning assumptions of Blind Logic were to serve as the intermediate step in alleviating the shortfalls in the post conflict phase.

Organizationally, the military did not initially structure forces to address the transition period. The lead agency for the post conflict operational phase was the Civil-Military Operations Task Force (CMOTF). CMOTFs assigned responsibilities included the civilian enabling functions in the post conflict environment. The primary planning assumption for the effectiveness of the CMOTF following the conflict phase was the deployment of civil affair units with specific skill sets to support the stability transition. However, the lack of an understanding of the post conflict environment and requirements necessary to facilitate the stability efforts quickly overwhelmed the capabilities of the CMOTF. It was unprepared and unable to address the massive looting, an ineffective transitional government and a societal breakdown in the transition period.[102]

One month after the invasion the U.S. Military Support Group – Panama (MSG) subsumed CMOTF. The MSG proved to be more effective. The ad-hoc organization quickly developed an integrative relationship with the reforming Panamanian government. Efforts to involve the populace in the decision making of stability efforts that nested with the political and societal norms proved to be effective.[103] The MSG devised a country team plan that outlined goals and objectives, integrated civilian agencies and expanded governmental reforms that nested with civic leaders.[104] Two months after the cessation of conflict, the integrated post conflict strategy was finally established.

---

[101]Ibid., 175.

[102]Shultz, *In the Aftermath of War*, xii.

[103]Ibid., 39-42.

[104]Ibid., 40.

Stakeholder Integration

The planning for the transition period should begin as early as feasible and continuously reassessed as the conflict evolves. This planning should be an integrated process that works towards an identified achievable end state. The transition period requires a shared civilian-military effort to properly assess, plan and implement effective measures towards the promotion of stability. In Operation Just Cause, the planning for the post conflict phase was missing an integrated and interagency effort to support the post conflict phase. The lack of interagency participation in the planning and execution of Operation Blind Logic handicapped the ability of the involved actors to respond to the events following the conflict.

Initially, operational planners considered creating an organizational structure similar to that implemented in the Vietnam intervention. The Civil Operations and Revolutionary Development Support Program (CORDS) was a military civilian joint planning model that focused on three organizational priorities to assist in stabilizing Southern Vietnam and mitigate insurgency. The first was to implement security, the second was to develop programs to increase population sentiment and the third was the large-scale implementation of efforts.[105] Of particular note to a review of the Panamanian involvement is that CORDS program unified the command structure of military and civilian agencies under one reporting authority unifying the expertise and resources of the U.S. interagency. However, policy and military planners in favor of a doctrinal military structure supporting conventional focused objectives ultimately threw out the CORDs model.[106] Despite previous lessons learned and the critical need for assisted planning for the civilian sector, the integration of the interagency community was ultimately ineffective.

---

[105]Dale Andrade and James Willbanks, "CORDS/Phoenix: Counterinsurgency Lessons from Vietnam for the Future," *Military Review* (March/April 2006): 11.

[106]Fishel, *The Fog of Peace: Planning and Executing the Restoration of Panama*, 74-75.

Operation Just Cause and Operation Blind Logic (Promote Liberty) would be a unilateral military effort.

Influence of Power and Culture

An effective evaluation of the influences of power and culture and the transition process involves an understanding of the historical and existing framework of conflict nation's government. This analysis can reveal the limitations and capabilities of societal and civic institutions and the possible responses in the post conflict period. The policy stated vision for the intervention in Panama was the defense of democracy. The broadly defined policy goal of restoring the democratic institutions was to prove problematic due in no small part to the historical foundations of democratic rule in Panama. In theory, the Panamanian government was a constitutional government and incorporated an electoral process dating back to 1903.[107] However, utilizing the criteria as outlined by political scientist, Samuel Huntington, the Panamanian democratic system did not even meet the minimal criteria of democratic rule in which the "most powerful collective decision makers are selected through fair, honest, and periodic elections in which virtually all the adult population is eligible to vote."[108] This characterization did not describe the civic environment in the Panamanian government. Historically and culturally, the influence of power resided in societal elements outside of the minimalist definition of a democratic nation.

The review of the historical tradition of the influence of power in Panama reveals two insights. The first is that political and military power resided in a select range of upper class

---

[107]Richard Millett, "Government and Politics," extracted from Sandra W. And Dennis M. Hanratty Meditz, *Panama: a Country Study,* (Washington DC: GPO, 1989), 174-83.

[108]Samuel P. Huntington, *The Third Wave: Democratization in the Late 20th Century* (Norman, OK: University of Oklahoma Press, 1993), 7.

families that utilized the military and police in leveraging political power.[109] The second is that

this military became in effect the decision maker in the political decisions of government and

arrested the development of civilian political parties and bureaucratic institutions.[110] The military

dominated governmental organization that repressed the integral elements of a liberal democracy

and the civic structure characterized the two previous decades. This was the operational

environment in the conflict period. In the post conflict transition, this power structure would

collapse and the ability and capabilities of the Panamanian society outside this structure were

unable to fill the void.

Post conflict stability enabling is not restricted to governmental support alone. In many

post conflict environments the civil society groups can provide an enabling capability in place of

a weakened or collapsed transitional state.[111] In the absence of functional governmental

institutions in the transition period, the intervening actors can enable civil society groups to

decrease levels of instability. In the example of Panama, the religious homogeneity throughout

the region may have provided an avenue for enabling societal control. This can provide localized

support to areas of the populace until enduring governmental institutions are functional.

The absence of a democratic tradition, a professional bureaucracy, a non-politicized

security and a society that was equipped to assume the mantle of governmental leadership all

contributed to the post conflict transitional instability. There is "little evidence to suggest that

those planning for restoration either realistically understood or adequately addressed historical

---

[109]John and Mavis Biesanz, *The People of Panama* (Westport, Conn.: Greenwood Press,London, 1977), 24.

[110]Richard H. Shultz, Jr.*, In the Aftermath of War: U.S. Support for Reconstruction and Nation-Building in Panama Following Just Cause* (Maxwell AFB, AL: Air University Press, 1993), 17.

[111]Daniel N. Posner, *Civil Society and the Reconstruction of Failed States*, extracted from *When States Fail: Cause and Consequences*, ed. Robert Rotberg (Princeton: Princeton University Press, 2004), 239.

and contextual issues.[112] The defeat of the PDF and the fall of the Noriega government gave way to a breakdown of population security functions and criminality immediately spiked. As existing security institutions dissolve, the transition environment often experiences a rise in crime and violence. The lack of preplanning and trained personnel in policing, engineering and civil affairs personnel frustrated immediate efforts to implement law enforcement measures and promote stability.[113] In the Panama intervention, the inability to preplan and reorient prioritization of efforts during the transition phase contributed to the subsequent rise in criminality and disorder. The historical indicators of dysfunctional civic institutions may have provided planners the foresight to ensure resources were in place to mitigate the shortfall.

In summary, the U.S. government and its agencies were conceptually and organizationally ill equipped for the transitional period in the Panamanian conflict. The focus on combat operations in the planning process and execution coupled with the inability to implement near term mitigation efforts delayed the effective transition to stability. The lack of a conceptual understanding of what defines transitions and the lack of a policy-guiding element contributed to the lack of response in implementing the most rudimentary elements of stability enhancing measures. Additionally, the lack of an integrated and interagency planning process that addressed political, economic and social aspects of the transitional period neglected short-term condition setting. Interagency and civilian assistance from other US governmental organizations was almost nonexistent due to their exclusion from the planning process that had initiated almost a year

---

[112]Shultz, Jr., *In the Aftermath of War*, 17.

[113]Fishel and Downie,"Taking Responsibility for Our Actions? Establishing Order and Stability in Panama," 70–75.

prior.[114] This lack of enabling support to a society that did not have the capability to perform

functions of government frustrated overall policy intents.

The lessons learned from the Panamanian intervention include the need to integrate

organizationally and conceptually with the interagency community. In addition to the identified

shortfalls in trained civil-military personnel, the U.S. military failed to approach the transition

process with a deliberate planning process that adequately addressed the transition period. The

identification on the primary influences of political and civil power lay in a historical review of

the loci of power influences in the nation of Panama. This analysis may have identified the need

for a directed and dedicated enforcement of all areas of civic control until enduring bureaucratic

and civil resources were developed.

ANALYSIS

Successful conflict termination consists of conducting early interagency planning,

establishing workable objectives, providing adequate intelligence, ensuring unity of effort,

integrating civil and military efforts and establishing the appropriate post conflict

organizations.[115] The pre transition planning and objectives are an important starting point for the

successful approach to the post conflict period. However, as the conflict will evolve the

environment these planning objectives must remain flexible. "Having an exit strategy on the shelf

at the beginning of hostilities and sticking to it until the end assumes away the potent influences

---

[114]Larry Yates, Robert Wright and Joe Huddleston, "Joint Task Force South in Operation Just Cause," (Oral History Interview of Lieutenant Gernaerla Carmen Cavessa conducted at Ft Lewis, Washington, 30 April, 1992). http://www.army.mil/cmh-pg/documents/panama/jcit/ JCIT97Z.htm (accessed on January 7, 2013).

[115]Fred Charles Iklé, *Every War Must End*, revised ed. (New York: Columbia University Press, 1991), 6-7.

of military performance on war aims as well as the law of intended political consequences that attends any major military intervention."[116]

Developing a better understanding and conceptual approach to the post conflict transition is vital for several reasons. First, the U.S. and the international community nation-building efforts have become more frequent with little indication that this trend will decline. Second, the post conflict transition hosts both opportunities and obstacles in setting the conditions for long-term stability efforts. An integrated and holistic approach that incorporates non-material considerations may alleviate the amount of resourcing and time that is required to implement enduring stability measures. Third, the capitalization of military successes and translating them into foreign policy end states will remain critical to U.S. and international security interests. Effectively transiting the security gap following conflict operations will facilitate this interest while minimizing risk to policy, populations and the legitimacy of that effort.

The complex environment of the transition period will continue to challenge effective implantation of methods enabling long-term stability. Culture and context is a non-fixed and fluid variable consisting of the elements of language, religion, social structures, traditions and value systems. The elements of power are tools to both implement and integrate shared visions of long-term stability efforts. The success of the transition will be dependent upon a holistic approach. An approach that must include the population influencers the ultimately involve a change in attitude among both the general populace and the disaffected spoilers. The influences of power and culture provide drivers that can facilitate acceptable outcomes of all stakeholders.

Transition efforts will continue to be ad hoc in nature as long as there remains unilateral stakeholder effort. As early as 2005, the Department of Defense has emphasized the importance

---

[116]Jeffrey Record, "Exit Strategy Decisions," *Parameters* 31 (Winter 2001–2002): 25.

of the ongoing effort to increase its capabilities at supporting stability in conflict-afflicted nations. "DoD is working to make stability operations a core competency of our armed forces."[117] However, despite the efforts of the military's intent to build its capacity to execute stability operations it should not be the preferred path. Numerous national and international agencies continue to produce ideas and methods in which to make the transition period comprehensively understandable and more manageable. This collaboration will increase the ability of planners to understand the complexity or interactions across political, social, military and economic dominions. The next step is to then integrate and incorporate all relevant stakeholders actively into the problem framing and solution building process. Then transitional stakeholders can actualize a shared vision that accommodates both intervening and intervened state policy goals. This may be the most promising avenue in which to integrate different institutions towards shared policy intent. U.S. military doctrine through the design and ADM constructs offer possibility to embrace an interdisciplinary construct to support operational planning.

Future efforts at expanding the conceptual tools and frameworks for the post conflict period will continue to improve upon the methodologies of transitional planning. While no single tool can realistically capture the specific complexity of transition, the integrative element of a collaborative framework can enable the transition processes. The military and civilian agencies transitional definitions and particular priorities limit the effectiveness of unilateral planning frameworks. Future study focusing on the foundational indicators and influencing factors that affect the society in transition may assist in a more comprehensive analysis of the post conflict period. This will assist in developing planning approaches that incorporate priorities in stability confidence measures rather than organizational lines of effort.

---

[117]Ryan Henry, Principal Deputy Under Secretary of Defense for Policy, "Prepared Statement for the Senate Foreign Relations Committee, 16 June 2006," http://foreign.senate.gov /hearings/2005/hrg05066a.html (accessed 3 November 2012).

CONCLUSION

An effective transition following military victories continues to challenge strategic and foreign policy goals. Since the conclusion of the Second World War, the U.S. and the international community have continued to seek approaches to better transition out of conflict and into long-term stability. "Strange as it may seem, the military victory is the easiest part of the struggle. After this has been attained, the real challenge begins: the reestablishment of a secure environment opens a new opportunity for nation building."[118] The transition period following conflict may be the most decisive temporal period in which to secure operational military gains and establish the conditions for long-term stability.

The common understanding of what characterizes a transition and the elements within it are a starting point for the necessary shared understanding amongst stakeholders. Planning and operational guidance in doctrine must incorporate an appreciation for the expanded definition of the interagency and academic community. Current doctrine emphasizes the need for early planning in transitioning to stability and population focused operations however, doctrinal and phasing guidance must enable operational commanders the ability to view the transition period in its own context and frame. The transition from conflict to stability is a distinct change in policy center of gravity. It is therefore vital that military doctrine incorporates an appreciation of the integral elements within the transition phase. In order to better prepare for the transition phase there must be an integrative approach by military and civilian planners in assessing and conceptually understanding the independent context of the post conflict transition.

The deliberate integration and shared vision of collaborating stakeholders is another fundamental criterion in capitalizing on the transition period. Reexamining and reassessing the transition period with a wider range of stakeholder begins with a communal understanding of

---

[118]George K. Tanham, *War without Guns: American Civilians in Rural Vietnam* (New York: Praeger, 1966), 138.

63

what characterizes the transition. The U.S. military planning in state interventions has demonstrated its capability in kinetic operations. The U.S interagency community must continue to seek ways in which to better integrate the operations and planning structures of stove piped institutions. This remains a serious shortfall in the overall ability to incorporate the larger body of stakeholders in post conflict planning. The U.S. and its international partners must continue to build upon historical lessons of interagency partnerships to improve upon organizational relationships. However, the most promising avenue is to promote and improve upon existing planning frameworks to provide the integrating element in transitional planning and shared understanding.

The enabling cognitive concepts that appreciate the motivating influences of a post conflict society additionally serve to facilitate an optimal transition. A post conflict transition that establishes favorable conditions for long-term stability is contingent upon implementation measures steeped in the historical elements of power and the driving forces of culture. The approach to conflict transition must emphasize a drastic reorientation of the elements of national and social power, micro and macro analysis of the post conflict social fabric and a critical review of current planning priorities. As the transition gap materializes, planning should be reassessed and cognitive frameworks reevaluated in the new contextual environment with consideration on how to leverage social and political institutions. This monograph offers a nuanced approach at developing an appreciation for the conceptual and systems approach at understanding these complex contextual environments. Future interagency and international professionals have the challenge to improve and expand upon these conceptual models in improving upon the comprehensive understanding of the transitional period.

The U.S. experiences in Panama and Iraq reveal the need for a greater collective understanding by all stakeholders of the transition period. The challenges transitioning from conventional combat operations to long-term stability efforts to achieve policy objectives are not without solutions. The temporal gap bridging conflict and peace provides an opportunity for all planners in the interagency and international community to implement effective and efficient measures that incorporate an appreciation for the deeper influencing elements of the society in transition.

There is no doubt that the U.S. governmental agencies and the international community will continue to pursue better methodologies and planning frameworks in future endeavors to stabilize post conflict nations. These transitions will continue to include unique contexts involving a broad range of stakeholders in the post conflict period. A holistic understanding of the unique and complex transition period, an integrated approach by all invested stakeholders and an appreciation of the influencing elements of history, power and culture within the society can facilitate these efforts. The one universal static element that will continue to bind the efforts and planning of all invested actors will be the desired outcome of a lasting and enduring stability for the nation emerging from conflict.

BIBLIOGRAPHY

Allison, Graham, and Philip Zelikow. *Essence of Decision: Explaining the Cuban Missile Crisis.* Second edition. New York: Longman, 1999.

Andrade, Dale, and James Willbanks. "CORDS/Phoenix: Counterinsurgency Lessons from Vietnam for the Future." *Military Review* (March/April 2006): 11.

Armstrong, Nicholas J., and Jacqueline Chura-Beaver. *Harnessing Post-Conflict.* Carlisle, PA: BiblioGov, 2012.

Arquilla, John, and David Ronfeldt. *The Emergence of Noopolitik: Toward an American Information Strategy.* Santa Monica, CA: Rand Publishing, 1999.

Ballentine, Karen. *Profiting from Peace: Managing the Resource Dimensions of Civil War.* Boulder: Lynne Rienner Publishers, 2005.

Bandali, Naveed. "Coordinating Reconstruction and Stabilization: An Interview with Ambassador John E. Herbst (Ret.)." *Journal of International Peace Operations* 6, no. 4 (January-February 2011).

Banach, Stefan J. "Educating By Design: Preparing Leaders for a Complex World." *Military Review* (March-April 2009): 97.

Bayley, David H. *Democratizing the Police Abroad: What to Do and How to Do It.* Washington, DC: U.S. Department of Justice, NCJ 188742, June 2001.

_____. "U.S. Aid for Foreign Justice and Police." *Orbis* 50, no. 3 (Summer 2006).

Benson, Kevin. "Phase IV: A Planner's Reply to Brigadier General Alywin-Foster."*Military Review,* (March-April 2006).

Betts, Richard. *Soldiers, Statesmen and Cold War Crises.* New York: Columbia University Press, 1991, original edition 1977.

Biesanz, John, and Mavis Biesanz. *The People of Panama.* Westport, CT: Greenwood Press, London, 1977.

Boule, John R. "Operational Planning and War Termination." *Joint Forces Quarterly,* (Autumn/Winter 2001–2002): 97-102.

Brown, Greg. *Learning to Leave: The Preeminence of Disengagement in US Military Strategy.* Drew Paper No. 3, Maxwell Air Force Base: Air University Press, 2008.

Buckley, Kevin. *Panama: The Whole Story.* New York: Simon & Schuster, 1991.

CBS News Archive. "Text of Bush Speech." *CBS News*, 1 May 2003. http://www.cbsnews.com/2100-500257_162-551946.html (accessed February 4, 2013).

Chan, Steve. "Exploring Puzzles in Power-Transitions Theory: Implications for Sino-American Relations," *Security Studies* 13, no. 3 (2004).

Clausewitz, Carl von. *On War.* Edited and translated by Michael Howard and Peter Paret. Princeton: Princeton University Press, 1984.

Clausewitz, Carl von. *Two Letters on Strategy.* Translated and edited by Peter Paret and Daniel Moran. Carlisle. PA: US Army War College, 1984.

Crane, Conrad C. "Phase IV Operations: Where Wars Are Really Won." *Military Review,* (May-June 2005): 27–36.

_____. *Landpower and Crises: Army Roles and Missions in Smaller-Scale Contingencies During the 1990s.* Carlisle, PA: Strategic Studies Institute, U.S. Army War College, January 2001.

Dacher, Keltner. "The Power Paradox." *Greater Good* (Winter 2007-2008): 15.

Dahl Robert A. *Who Governs: Democracy and Power in an American City.* New Haven, CT: Yale University Press, 1961.

DeToy, Brian. *Turning Victory into Success: Military Operations after the Campaign.* Ft. Leavenworth: Combat Studies Institute, September 2004.

Dobbins, James. *The Beginner's Guide to Nation-Building.* Santa Monica, CA: RAND Corporation, 2007.

Dodge, Toby. *Inventing Iraq: the Failure of Nation Building and a History Denied.* New York: Columbia University Press, 2005.

Doughtery, James E. *Contending Theories of International Relations: A Comprehensive Survey.* New York: Addison Wesley Longman, Inc, 1996.

Edelstein, David. "Exit Lessons." *Wilson Quarterly* 33 (Autumn 2009): 34–39.

_____. *Occupational Hazards: Success and Failure in Military Occupation.* Ithaca: Cornell University Press, 2008.

Fallows, James. "Blind into Baghdad." *The Atlantic Monthly* (January/February 2004).

Feaver, Peter. *Armed Servants: Agency, Oversight, and Civil-Military Relations.* Cambridge, MA: Harvard University Press, 2003.

Feaver, Peter, and Christopher Gelpi. *Choosing Your Battles: American Civil-Military Relations and the Use of Force.* Princeton: Princeton University Press, 2004.

Fishel, John T. *Civil Military Operations in the New World.* Westport, CT: Praeger Publisher, 1997.

_____. *The Fog of Peace: Planning and Executing the Restoration of Panama.* Carlisle Barracks, PA: USAWC Strategic Studies Institute, April 1992.

Fishel, John, and Richard Downie. "Taking Responsibility for Our Actions? Establishing Order and Stability in Panama." *Military Review* (April 1992).

Franks, Tommy, and Malcolm McConnell. *American Soldier*. New York: Harper Collins, 2004.

Forman, Johanna M. *Inevitable Conflicts, Avoidable Failures: Preparing for the Third Generation of Conflict, Stabilization, and Reconstruction Operations*. Washington, DC: Center for Strategic and International Studies, July 2012.

Gray, Colin S. *Hard Power and Soft Power: the Utility of Military Force as an Instrument of Policy in the 21st Century*. Carlisle, PA: CreateSpace Independent Publishing Platform, 2012.

Gregor, William J. "War Termination in the Age of Terror: Searching for a Dialogue." Paper presented at the biennial conference of the Inter-University Seminar on Armed Forces and Society, Chicago, IL, 26 October 2007.

Hammes, Thomas X. *The Sling and the Stone: On War in the 21st Century*. St. Paul, MN: Zenith Press, 2004.

Henry, Ryan. Principal Deputy Under Secretary of Defense for Policy, "Prepared Statement for the Senate Foreign Relations Committee, 16 June 2006." http://foreign.senate.gov /hearings/2005/hrg05066a.html (accessed 3 November 2012).

Herbst, Jeffrey. *Learning from Somalia: The Lessons of Armed Humanitarian Intervention*. Boulder: Westview Press, 1997.

Huntington, Samuel. *The Soldier and the State: The Theory and Politics of Civil-Military Relations*. Cambridge, MA: Harvard University Press, 1998.

Huntington, Samuel P. *The Third Wave: Democratization in the Late 20th Century*. Norman, OK: University of Oklahoma Press, 1993.

Ikenberry, G. John. *After Victory: Institutions, Strategic Restraint, and the Rebuilding of Order After Major Wars*. Princeton: Princeton University Press, 2001.

Iklé, Fred Charles. *Every War Must End*. Rev. ed. New York: Columbia University Press, 1991.

Jones, Seth G. *Establishing Law and Order After Conflict*. Santa Monica, CA: Rand Publishing, 2005.

Kalyvas, Stathis N. *The Logic of Violence in Civil War*. Cambridge University Press, 2006.

Katzman, Kenneth. *Afghanistan: Post-Taliban Governance Security, and U.S. Policy*. Washington, DC: Congressional Research Service (CRS) RL30588, 15 April 2011.

Kelly, Terrence K, Seth G. Jones, James E. Barnett II, Keith Crane, Robert C. Davis, and Carl Jensen, eds.. *A Stability Police Force for the United States: Justification and Options for Creating U.S. Capabilities*. Santa Monica, CA: RAND Corporation, 2009.

Kim, Sung Hee, and Pruitt, Dean. *Social Conflict: Escalation, Stalemate and Settlement*. McGraw Hill, 1994.

Kleisner, Theodore W. "Disengagement Operations: Context, Violence, and Spoilers in a New Phase IV Construct." Monograph, US Army School of Advanced Military Studies, 2010.

Kupchan, Charles, Jason Davidson, and Mira Sucharov. *Power in Transition: The Peaceful Change of International Order*. Tokyo, Japan New York: United Nations University Press, 2001.

Lawson, Brooke S, Terrence K. Kelly, Michelle Parker, Kimberly Colloton, and Jessica Watkins. *Reconstruction Under Fire: Case Studies and Further Analysis of Civil Requirements*. Santa Monica, CA: RAND Corporation, 2010.

Lederach, John Paul. *Building Peace: Sustainable Reconciliation in Divided Society*. Washington, DC: United States Institute for Peace, 1997.

Leaning, Jennifer, and Sam Arie. "Human Security: A Framework for Assessment in Conflict and Transition." *Tulane University/CERTI initiative* (December 2010): 4.

Levite, Ariel E. *Foreign Military Intervention: The Dynamics of Protracted Conflict*. New York: Columbia University Press, 1992.

Licklider, Roy. *Stopping the Killing: How Civil Wars End*. New York: New York University Press, 1993.

Lukes, Steven. *Power: A Radical View*, 2nd ed. London: Palgrave Macmillian, 2005.

Mandel, Robert. *The Meaning of Military Victory*. London: Lynne Rienner Publishers, 2006.

Marshall, Monty G, and Benjamin R. Cole. *Global Report 2009: Conflict, Governance and State Fragility*. George Mason University: Centers for Systematic Peace, 2009.

Massoud, Tansa George. "War Termination." *Journal of Peace Research* 33, no. 4 (November 1996): 491–496.

McDonnell, Janet A. After *Desert Storm: The U.S. Army and the Reconstruction of Kuwait* (Washington, DC: Government Printing Office, 1999), 32.

Millett, Richard Millett. "Government and Politics," extracted from Sandra W. and Dennis M. Hanratty Meditz, *Panama: a Country Study (area Handbook Series)*. Washington, DC: Government Printing Office.

Murray, Williamson, and Major General Robert H. Scales, Jr. *The Iraq War: A Military History*. Cambridge, MA: Belknap Press of Harvard University Press, 2003.

National Security Archive. "The Future of Iraq Project Report: Working Group Recommendations," November 2002. http://www.gwu.edu/~nsarchiv/NSAEBB/ NSAEBB198/index.htm (accessed 14 March 2013).

Nagel, Jack. *The Descriptive Analysis of Power*. New Haven, CT: Yale University Press, 1975.

Newman, Edward. *The Impact of Spoilers on Peace Processes and Peacebuilding,* Policy Report no. 2. Tokyo: United Nations University, 2006.

New York Times. "A Transcript of President Bush's Address on the Decision to Use Force, 21 December 1989." http://www.nytimes.com/1989/12/21/world/fighting-panama-president-transcript-bush-s-address-decision-use-force-panama.html (accessed on 13 December 2012).

Nye, Joseph S. *The Future of Power.* Public Affairs: Perseus Books Group, 2011.

Nye, Joseph. *Soft Power: The Means to Success in World Politics.* New York: Public Affairs, 2005.

Oakley, Robert. *Somalia and Operation RESTORE HOPE: Reflections on Peacemaking and Peacekeeping.* Washington, DC: United States Institute of Peace, 1995.

Office of Inspector General. *Management of Homeland Security International Activities and Interests, OIG–08–71.* Washington, DC: U.S. Department of Homeland Security, June 2008.

Office of the Secretary of Defense. *Sustaining U.S. Global Leadership: Priorities for 21st Century Defense* (5 January 2012): 4. www.defense.gov/news/Defense_Strategic_Guidance.pdf (accessed 20 November 2012).

Posner, Daniel N. *Civil Society and the Reconstruction of Failed States.* Extracted from *When States Fail: Cause and Consequences,* ed. Robert Rotberg. Princeton: Princeton University Press, 2004.

Presidential Decision Directive. National Security Council 56, Managing Complex Contingency Operations. www.fas.org/irp/offdocs/pdd56/htm (accessed 4 February 2013), 2-3.

Record, Jeffrey. "Exit Strategy Delusions." *Parameters* (Winter 2001-2002): 21-27.

Ricks, Thomas E. *Fiasco: the American Military Adventure in Iraq, 2003 to 2005.* Reprint. New York: Penguin Books, 2007.

Rosenau, William. *Low-Cost Trigger Pullers: The Politics of Policing in the Context of Contemporary "State Building" and "Counterinsurgency."* Santa Monica, CA: RAND Working Paper, October 2008.

Rubinstein, Robert A., Diana M. Keller, and Michael E. Scherger. "Culture and interoperability in integrated Missions." *International Peacekeeping* 15, no.4 (2008): 540–555.

Samuels, Richard. *Securing Japan: Tokyo's Grand Strategy and the Future of East Asia.* Ithaca: Cornell, 2007.

Secretary of Defense. *Report to Congress on the Implementation of DODD 3000.05 Military Support for Stability, Security, Transition, and Reconstruction (SSTR) Operations.* (Washington, DC: Government Printing Office, 2007), i.

Senge, Peter M. *The Fifth Discipline: the Art and Practice of the Learning Organization*, revised ed. New York: Doubleday, 2006.

Serafino, Nina M. *Peacekeeping/Stabilization and Conflict Transitions: Background and Congressional Action On the Civilian Response/reserve Corps and Other Civilian Stabilization and Reconstruction Capabilities.* Washington, DC: Congressional Research Service, 2012.

Shambach, Stephen A., ed. *Strategic Leadership Primer*, 2nd ed. Carlisle Barracks, PA: U.S. Army War College, 2004.

Shanker, Thom. "Defense Secretary Urges More Spending for U.S. Diplomacy." *New York Times,* 27 November 2007.

Shultz, Richard H. *In the Aftermath of War: U.S. Support for Reconstruction and Nation-Building in Panama Following Just Cause.* Ann Arbor: University of Michigan Library, 1993.

Snyder, Jack. *The Ideology of the Offensive: Military Decision Making and the Disasters of 1914.* Ithaca: Cornell, 1984.

Solberg, Carl Arthur. *Culture and Industrial Buyer Behavior: The Arab Experience.* Dijon, France, September 2002.

Soysa, Indra De, John Oneal, and Yee-Hee Park. "Testing Power-Transition Theory Using Alternative Measure of National Capabilities," *The Journal of Conflict Resolution,* 41, no.4 (1977).

Strachan, Hew. "Strategy or Alibi? Obama, McChrystal, and the Operational Level of War." *Survival* 52:5 (2010): 440.

Tabor, Robert. *War of the Flea: The Classic Study of Guerrilla Warfare.* Washington, DC: Brassey's, Inc, 2002.

Tanham, George K. *War without Guns: American Civilians in Rural Vietnam.* New York: Praeger, 1966.

Terril, Andrew W. *Precedents, Variables, and Options in Planning a U.S. Military Disengagement Strategy from Iraq.* Carlisle: Strategic Studies Institute, 2005.

U.S. Army. Army Doctrine Publication (ADP) 3–0, *Unified Land Operations.* Washington DC: Government Printing Office, October 2011.

_____. Army Doctrine Publication (ADP) 3–07, *Stability.* Washington, DC: Government Printing Office, August 2012.

_____. Army Doctrine Publication (ADP) 5–0, *The Operations Process.* Washington, DC: Government Printing Office, May 2012.

_____.Army Doctrine Reference Publication (ADRP) 3–0, *Unified Land Operations.* Washington, DC: Government Printing Office, May 2012.

_____. Army Doctrine Reference Publication (ADRP) 5–0, *The Operations Process.* Washington, DC: Government Printing Office, May 2012.

_____. Field Manual (FM) 3–24, *Counterinsurgency.* Washington, DC: Government Printing Office, 15 December 2006.

_____. Field Manual (FM) 3–07, *Stability Operations.* Washington, DC: Government Printing Office, 2008.

_____. TP 525-5-500, *Commander's Appreciation and Campaign Design.* Fort Monroe, VA: US Army Training and Doctrine Command, 28 January 2008.

U.S. Army Training and Doctrine Command/CSI 2004 Conference. *Turning Victory Into Success: Two Centuries of American Campaigning.* Fort Leavenworth KS: CSI Press, 2004.

U.S. Department of Defense. Joint Forces Command, Futures Group. *The Joint Operating Environment 2009: Update Challenges and Implications for the Future Joint Force.* Norfolk: Joint Forces Command, 2009.

U.S. Department of Defense. *The Joint Staff. Joint Staff Special Historical Study: Operation JUST CAUSE, Planning and Execution of Joint Operations in Panama February 1988-January 1990.* Washington, DC: Government Printing Office, December 1990.

———. Department of Defense Instruction (DODI) 3000.05, *Stability Operations.* Washington, DC: Government Printing Office, September 2009.

———. Joint Publications (JP) 3–0, *Joint Operations.* Washington, DC: Government Printing Office, 2006.

——— . Joint Publications (JP) 5–0, *Joint Operation Planning.* Washington, DC: Government Printing Office, 2006.

———. Joint Publications (JP) 3–07, *Stability Operations.* Washington, DC: Government Printing Office, 29 September 2011.

U.S. Department of Defense News. "Dempsey: Iraq Campaign Was worth the Cost," (15 December 2011): 1. http://www.defense.gov/news/newsarticle.aspx?id=66488 (accessed 4 February 2013).

U.S. Department of State, "S/CRS Fact Sheet." www.state.gove/s/crs/rls/43327.htm (accessed 22 October 2012).

_____. "Quadrennial Diplomacy and Development Review," 2010. http://www.state.gov/documents/organization/15310.pdf (accessed 4 November 2012), 136.

_____. "White House applauds results of Iraqi opposition conference," 17 December 2002. http://war-in-iraq.diktaali.net/links/zip/U_S_%20Department% 20of%20State%20-%20Future%20of%20Iraq.htm (accessed 12 November 2013).

U.S. Joint Chiefs of Staff. *National Military Strategy of the United States*, Washington, DC: Government Printing Office, 1997.

United Nations. *Report to the Secretary General on Humanitarian Needs in Iraq by a Mission Led by Sadruddin Aga Khan, Executive Delegate of the Secretary General,* New York: 15 July, 1991. http://www.casi.org.uk/info/undocs/s22799.html (accessed 1 March 2013).

United States Institute of Peace. "Guiding Principles for Stabilization and Reconstruction (SSR)." *UNDP/WB, Draft Joint Guidance Note on Integrated Recovery Planning* (2009): 5–32, http:www.state.gov/j/cso/resources (accessed 16 November 2012).

United States Special Operations Command. Memorandum for Commander in Chief, U.S. Southern Command, ATTN: J3, Quarry Heights, Panama, *Subject: Organization of Nation Building Forces,* 1-2.UNDP Human Development Report 2010. http://hdr.undp.org/en/media/HDR_2010_EN_Complete.pdf. (accessed on 4 February, 2013).

Wallace, William Scott, LTG. Interview for *Frontline: invasion of Iraq,* available at http://www.pbs.org/wgbh/pages/frontline/shows/invasion/interviews/ wallace.html (accessed 13 Junuary 2013).

Wunderle, William D. *Through the Lens of Cultural Awareness*. New York: BiblioGov, 2012.

Yates, Larry, Robert Wright, and Joe Huddleston. "Joint Task Force South in Operation Just Cause." Oral History Interview of Lieutenant Gernaerla Carmen Cavessa conducted at Fort Lewis, Washington, 30 April 1992. http://www.army.mil/cmh-pg/documents/panama/jcit/ JCIT97Z.htm (accessed on 7 January 7, 2013).

Zinni Lt. Gen. Anthony. "Lt. Gen. Zinni's Twenty Lessons Learned for Humanitarian Assistance and Peace Operations." Presented at the Center for Naval Analysis Annual Conference Proceedings: Military Support to Complex Humanitarian Emergencies, (1995), 5.